Puzzle Peace

Living the Abundant Life

In the Age of Anxiety

Alan H. Collier

GTD PUBLISHING

ISBN 978-0692968741

POWAY, CA - December, 2017

CONTENTS

♦ 1 ♦

Al the Kiddies' Pal

Like many attorneys I know, I never really wanted to be a lawyer. My dad was an art teacher, my older brother was an English teacher, my sister was a social worker, and my younger brother was clearly focused on carrying on my dad's artist mantel – which he has as an art professor in Vermont. I was not an overly driven worker, but rather got by on the brains I inherited from my mother, and spent as much time as possible having adventures, reading about adventures, or playing. I never learned to golf and didn't like it when I tried later in life (when I was forced to since it was a major part of client promotion as a lawyer). I didn't, and don't, like confrontation and avoid it at all cost. To cap it all off, I really wasn't interested in prestige, power, or becoming wealthy. All I really wanted was to be a good husband and have an abundant marriage like my parents (which I have), to be a good father and enjoy my kids at every age (which I have), and to have fun and a lot of adventures (which I have).

I've had a number of nicknames in my life, but one that stuck (started by my little brother) is "Al the Kiddies' Pal" which I picked up as I inherited my dad's knack for entertaining kids. Whether it's making up silly games (like lick-wedgie, porky-sush, or daddyator), hunting for bull frogs, going tee-peeing, or telling slightly off-color jokes which sometimes got me in trouble, I always kept my kids, my friends' kids and my kid's friends laughing and having fun - not only to bring them joy - but also because it's so fun.

So, how does Al the Kiddies' Pal become an equity partner in a big New York/Los Angeles law firm litigating cases all over the United States and across the world. Well, when I went to college at Abilene Christian University in Texas, I thought I wanted to be an artist like my dad - then an architect - then a pastor - then a teacher.

Nothing stuck until I started taking political science classes which finally got my brain working in a way that challenged me for the first time. I was hooked. But what do you do with a BA in political science? The answer - you teach (which I didn't want to do), or you become a City Manager (which I didn't want to do after interning in the 6,000 population oil town of Seminole, Texas where the City Manager began every City Council meeting facing a vote as to whether he would keep his job for that week or not), and being a lawyer. I wasn't opposed to being a lawyer; I just didn't ever want a "sell your soul to the devil" job, and I had no idea how I could ever pay for law school.

One day when I was coming out of the campus library, I saw a sign advertising a full scholarship to Pepperdine University Law School in Malibu, California. It so happened that Pepperdine was looking to have quality Christian students attend its law school and established the scholarship the year before at its sister school to that end. Well, after living in West Texas for four years, the pictures of the Malibu surf, together with my lack of direction, was all I needed. My beautiful blonde fiancé Libby was game to start our life in California where she had some family, so I went for it, and as the first piece in a complicated life puzzle, I got the scholarship and we were off to the West Coast to begin a new adventure.

Despite my academic success in college, as I walked on campus at Pepperdine, with all the beautiful and sharply dressed students, my insecurity began. Sure, I could succeed in small Abilene, Texas, but this was different - these were the best and the brightest, and all of them (at least in my filtered eyes) looked like future lawyers. Not me - I was just goofy and awkward Al the Kiddies' Pal. This insecurity (that would follow me into my legal career) was so powerful that when a professor compelled our first year class to make sure to take a break from studies on Sunday morning to read the newspaper (intimating that law school would require my attention for the other 95 percent of the week), I just "knew" this was not for me. Thank God, my young wife urged me to talk to someone. That someone was Professor LaGard Smith who wisely counseled me to ignore what everyone else said to do, and to focus on what got me to this point. If that didn't work after the first set of grades came out, then I could reassess my situation. In light of the fact this was all free, it would be foolish to just walk away. So, I began my law school career doing it the Al the Kiddies' Pal way by going to class and taking good notes, but then taking off the rest of the day to cook, read, play basketball and hang out with my lovely bride. The studying could wait until the next morning. Lo and behold, the Smith plan worked - I aced my first wave of tests, and lawyer Alan was off and running - not staying up all night with study groups, but rather making gourmet dinners, exploring beautiful Southern California, playing with my twin niece and nephew and generally having the time of my life.

My relaxed law school plan worked so well, I not only graduated with honors, but landed the only job I applied for - at the Los Angeles litigation office of a large New York insurance defense firm that my best friend had clerked for the summer before. My friend didn't accept their offer for a full-time position as he wanted to be a plaintiff's lawyer. He thought it would be perfect for me as it was family oriented due to the influence of a wonderful man who had moved from New York to start a new life after returning from Vietnam, then tragically losing his young wife to cancer. He now had a new lovely wife and son in California that he was determined to spend quality time with.

Now that I had a real job as a lawyer, and a set of twins to support, I decided that the only way I could survive was to show up early every day, fully immerse myself into my work while I was there, but leave every day at 5:00, catch the 5:30 train home and be with my young and growing family by 7:00. Then, I could not only have dinner with them, but also play, read stories and love on my kids, before having a home "date-night" with my wife. While my legal career took me all over the world (meaning I was often away from the family), when I was back in California, I was not only home every day at 7:00, but never (and I mean never) went into the office on a weekend in 25 years as a litigation lawyer. I was always home, doing what my art teacher father did - spending time with and loving on my family. I truly believe that this legacy passed on by my father is why my now four adult children are fun, stable, and know who they are - not only children of a loving earthly father, but a Heavenly Father who they live their life for.

Even though I went on to become the youngest partner ever made in a now 100 year old firm, and found favor with clients who appreciated the fact that I was an atypical attorney, my story isn't full of all happiness and joy. By the time I approached my 25th year as a lawyer, and my family-oriented partners had begun to lose power, I was so riddled with fear, insecurity and anxiety, that I became totally incapacitated. But that wasn't the end of the story. It was only another piece in the puzzle.

♦ 2 ♦

"The Killing Fields"

It's not heart attacks, it's not pornography, it's not depression, it's not nervous breakdowns, it's not divorce, it's not infidelity, it's not alcoholism, it's not isolation, it's not narcissism, it's not materialism, it's not apathy - these are not the things that are bringing down the men of our country (and many women with it as well) - it is what I believe causes each of them - ANXIETY.

We can't avoid it. We are taught from our earliest days as young boys that to succeed in life is to work tirelessly, go to college and beyond to earn the highest degree possible, make a lot of money, and obtain powerful positions in business, politics or the church. These are all ok things in and of themselves, and are often part of God's plan for our lives, but instead of being a tool for the Kingdom, they have become counterfeit gods. When we worship them (i.e., put our worth, hope and identity in them), they will surely fail us. The result is finding ourselves in a deep hole that is very hard to crawl out of.

I was blessed. I had a dad who wanted to support his family - and he did - but he never wanted what the world had to offer. While many of my other friend's dads were rarely seen as they worked long hours, came home exhausted and depleted of all emotional points, and then either worked or golfed on the weekends, my dad was different. He was always home before dark, always there for dinner with the family, always ready to engage with me and my siblings, and always focused on loving on my mom. I wanted to be the same, and I did everything in my power to be the dad to my kids that my dad was to me. This was going to be tough in the profession I had chosen which is nicknamed "the jealous mistress" for good reason. I was a litigation lawyer with clients and cases all over the world. It was super exciting and fulfilling. It was also a huge trap.

When I started, I thought I was ready. I vowed to be "different" and I was. It's hard to be believe looking back, but when I took my legal internship job at my firm in the summer of my 2nd year at Pepperdine, I actually told my workaholic boss we called Fitz (a man I grew to love dearly) that I needed to leave at 4:00 pm every day or I would get stuck in traffic and not have time to spend with my wife. My caveat was that I vowed to come in at 7:00 am every day. I found out later as I lived in the lawyer world for a time, that this was unheard of for a clerk trying to win over his potential employer. Well, despite myself, I worked hard and was one of only two summer clerks hired out of seven and found myself in a place I'd never imagined - on the upper floor of a high rise in downtown Los Angeles working for a big law firm.

My "different" life continued as my young family grew and by the time I was 32, I had four children under five years old. I traveled ALOT, worked hard, but always put my family first. I was always out the door and on the train home by 5:30 pm - with my beautiful wife and kids by 7:00 pm - and the one hour train journey gave me time to relax, read a book, nap, play cribbage with my friend Kipp, and ready myself to be a dad and husband when I got home. I never worked as many hours as the partners over me or my peers fighting to be partners someday, but I really believe that God blessed the prayer my friend Larry told me to always pray. On my first day as an intern, he told me that I was destined to be intimidated by the big building and fancy suits - destined to believe the lie that I didn't belong – but that God was in this and that I should pray for His favor EVERY DAY He blessed me with this special calling. That is something I did for 25 years. I prayed. Not only for God's favor as I walked through the door, but as I was always the first one in the office, to walk around and touch every door and ask for God's anointing on the place I worked. These were God's children. This was His firm.

It's way too long a story, but I did receive God's favor - not only in my family, where I had a beautiful marriage and children who loved God and were smart and fun - not only in our work for the Kingdom where Libby's non-profit TURN flourished and blessed our city and the world - but also at work where I rose above my "warrior" peers and became partner. I had done it the "right" way - so why did it go so wrong.

Satan is very clever - and persistent. I have battled insecurity for my whole life. I've discovered that a lot of men suffer the same problem. Whatever success we achieve, there is a little boy in us that still feels like we are a fake - that someone will find us out - that we've just gotten "lucky". This lie from the enemy works so well because our sin nature wants to take God off the throne and climb on. Once we are consumed with how "we" got there - based upon worldly traits like hard work, or brains, or good looks, or charisma, we tend to crash emotionally when our world of achievement starts to crumble even in the smallest way - or even just in our imagination. This is what happened to me. As much as I "thought" I trusted God, and as much as I said the right things about the favor I had achieved, I still listened to that voice inside (as well as the worldly voices around me) that told me I was the smartest person they knew, or that I looked like Richard Gere, or that I was the only guy they knew who actually balanced family and work in the perfect way. It's great to hear those things until you start believing that those things are the reason for your favor - because when the favor seems to leave, you start believing the lie again that all that has happened to bring you where you are is just a sham - a smoke screen that is beginning to clear.

I began to listen to that lie again when I made partner at my law firm. I wasn't worthy. I wasn't capable of being a leader. I wasn't the man my older partners were, who worked so hard and had achieved so much. I was just Al the Kiddies' Pal who wanted to get home as soon as he could to play with his kids and have a date with his wife. God had put me where I was but I was so focused on my insecurity, as well as my jealous peers (who actually did want me to fail), that I began to become blinded to the real truth. All my skill, all my intelligence, all my charisma, all my confidence, all my discernment - all the things that had made me a young equity partner in a large international law firm - were gifts from God to equip me for the greater purpose He had called me to.

Over the course of the next 13 years I did have moments where I walked in God's power and confidence - doing law by the Spirit, but I also succumbed to the darts of the enemy. These attacks came through jabs from colleagues or clients that should have drawn me into full reliance of God as my defender, but instead lured me into the trap of self-reliance and insecurity. The battle raged on not only in my mind, but also in those now in power who had never liked how I did things to begin with and began working behind the scenes to take me down a notch, if not out of the game entirely. When it all came to a head, it was clearly time to shut it down. I really believe God had called me to this life for the last 25 years, but it was time to do something new and escape the stress.

The problem with all this is that despite my newfound dissatisfaction with my work environment, I made a lot of money doing in that world. I was free from the rat race, but now faced an enormous wave of financial issues with college costs, a mortgage, and unbelievable tax debt without the ability to pay. I was only 50, but my confidence had been so shaken over the last few years that I couldn't imagine what I could do to make money. I had worked in the same job for 25 years in a very specialized field that I had no intention of jumping back into. My world had been rocked, and I was like a house built on sand.

Anxiety is a powerful thing. It causes heart problems, digestive issues, headaches, sexual dysfunction and worst of all depression. It is a lethal killer. It is Satan's tool to take out men (and many women) of influence through either horrible and destructive life decisions or physical illness. The more I reach out to pastors and businessmen, the more I realize how pervasive this problem is. The constant stress of this world (which is now 24/7 with the advent of technology) is literally killing men that God has a great plan for. The problem is that we become so entangled in the things of this world, we can't escape unless we literally crash.

In my darkest days I was depressed, hopeless, losing weight from lack of appetite, unable to be a husband to my wife or dad to my kids - I was a shell of what I was because of the cloud of anxiety I was surrounded by. Many reading this book may well be in the same place, or on their way there, but I am here to say that there is hope. God is there. He's holding you. He'll pull you out of the pit, but you have to reach out, you have to surrender all that the world says is important, and you have to find your identity in Christ and

Him alone. Then, it will all come back to you as it did for me. It was hard. It was humbling. My wife and friends had to rise up and send me to a place where I could find myself again. But even though God didn't want me to go through all the pain my family and I have had to endure in those dark months, "WOW" did He do something special out of the ashes! Jubilee is now here for me at age 50 and I can't wait for each new day to see what God has in store.

♦ 3 ♦

Sideways Walking Dogs

I have a dear friend whose name is Fred. Fred has had the most chaotic, difficult, jaw dropping life of anyone I have ever met. It is also the most God breathed. He grew up in a wealthy home in Orange County, California as the son of a contractor who owned his own construction business. His life should have been set to just work with his brothers and dad, someday lead the company and live a comfortable life. But there was another path for my buddy.

Fred and his brother Pete got bored and started dabbling in drugs and abusing alcohol. This led to a new career for the brothers – not in their father's business - but in dealing drugs out of their new home in Lake Elsinore, California. These were dark days, but now Fred was hooked and couldn't get out. When he ran out of money, he resorted to selling his body to older women as a male prostitute and kept sinking and sinking. He would eventually fall hard and end up not only "on" the streets of Los Angeles, but "under" them. You may not know this, but Los Angeles has a river running though the heart of the city, aptly named the Los Angeles River. It is not beautiful. In fact, it is a concrete wash to handle flood waters during heavy rains and is covered in graffiti from start to finish. If you saw the movie Grease, the Los Angeles River is where John Travolta has a drag race in his car "Greased Lightning."

The Los Angeles River has giant outlets all the way down its course in order to flow water into the "river" during times of heavy rain. Since "it never rains in California" the river is mostly dry, as are these outlets which are connected to a large and extensive underground network of tunnels. This is where Fred lived. This is where only the hardest and toughest of the homeless community in Los Angeles dare to go. The police don't even go there. Since Fred is a walking giant at 6 foot 5 and up to 300 pounds at times, he could handle himself, but this was not the life God had for Fred.

After a few years of life on the streets, he became ill and thought he was going to die. In his desperation, he laid on a park bench near Union Station and cried out to God to either let him die, or to pull him out of the pit and save him. Well, his mother's years of praying for her middle son were answered, the sky fell out with rain, and Fred was reborn as he committed his new life to serving God. He enrolled in a program called Teen Challenge where he was not only able to break his drug addiction, but also to learn that he was loved by God who had a hope and a future for him. Fred went on to attend Teen Challenge Ministry School and is currently a street pastor in Yreka, California. He has birthed a new Teen Challenge in this poor, drug-filled community in Northern California where he is saving his old self.

I don't know why it works this way, but for some reason we don't accept the fact that we "really" need to surrender to God until something devastating happens in our life. I don't think God intended it this way. I think He sends warnings and whispers to guide us down the right path of fully relying on Him versus the world, but we are so hard headed, a monster fall is the only way to wake us up to our need for Kingdom living. These "dark nights of the soul" don't happen because God wants to punish us, but rather because he loves us so much. He will literally do/allow anything to get us to realize our need for Him and the pathway to a truly fulfilling life here on earth. He rarely "causes" our pain, but rather takes the difficulties we think or walk our way into, and, after a time in the valley, reaches down and asks us if we are "finally" ready to take Daddy's hand and walk in the way He always intended.

This is what happened to Fred. I don't know of anyone who has been through, and continues to go through, more than he has. He lost his best friend and brother, together with his beloved nephew, when they were literally burned to death after a blown drug deal. He has suffered the insecurity, confusion and instability that comes with battling mental illness - an after effect of his drug addiction. His sister was kidnapped into sex slavery and was so badly abused that her body was never the same again. He continually battles physical ailments in his back and legs.

Yet, God took all these "bad" things and has lifted Fred out of the pit and made him a mighty warrior in the Kingdom. Fred is a walking Billy Graham crusade. Everywhere he goes he tells people about the love of Jesus! Whether it's a homeless man living in a box in the river bottom, a drug addict looking for his next hit, or a mom in a grocery store, he engages them and brings the Kingdom down to touch their lives. He knows who he is. He is a broken vessel that God has adopted and empowered to advance the work of Christ and fight back the work of the devil.

I don't know what it is about Fred, but because he is so full of the Spirit, crazy things happen to him all of the time, and when I say crazy, I mean crazy. The only way I can believe his impossible stories is that I was either there to witness them, or he has a scar or a claw (more in a minute) to prove them true.

As to the claw - well, one day Fred was driving his car through the remote mountains of Northern California in the Klamath National Forest when he felt a huge bump. When he got out of his truck, he saw a large brown bear laid out on the road. Yes, he had killed the California state animal (or so he thought). In his sadness for killing such a beautiful creature, he walked up to it as if to pay this king of the forest a tribute. The problem was that while his truck knocked the bear down and out, it was far from dead. When he nudged the bear with his foot, it quickly rolled over, and swiped Fred's legs from under him knocking him to the ground. While Fred is a large man, the bear was close to 400 pounds and easily pinned him down clawing away.

While most of us would have passed out from fright, Fred has not only lived a life under the streets, but also a time in prison. He knows how to survive. Time slowed down as he smelled the bear's warm breath on his face, felt the crush of his body, and the sting of his claws in his legs and torso. In a move that would make Jack Bauer proud, he reached out his hand, felt a rock the size of a softball, gripped it tight and whacked that bear in the side of the head so hard it knocked him out for the second time that day. This time Fred was a little wiser and booked it back to his car only to see the bear wake up and head to the woods with its tail between its legs. After a deep breath and some thank you Lords, Fred looked at his lower body and noticed that the bear had clawed straight through his jeans and into his leg. As he examined the wound, he felt something hard that had not been there before. He tugged and tugged, and when it finally came out, he had a two inch bear claw in his hand. This "trophy" of Fred's encounter with the bear is now a necklace that my daughter Becky wears to remind her that her second father Fred loves her, but that with God's strength and peace, no obstacle is too big or too fierce to overcome.

Now to the title of this chapter - Fred and I are brothers and best friends. He loves me and my family so much he would literally die for us. Since we are so close, we have lived through the ups and downs of life together. He is always the encouraging voice on the other end of the phone when I'm anxious and I've been able to see him through many rough days when he loses his way. During this journey through life together, there was a period of time where both of us were delivered from things in our lives that had gripped us for far too long. When the freedom came, the Holy Spirit showed up in a way I had never experienced before. It's hard to describe, but somehow God began to show both of us manifestations of the spirit world in the physical. Hawks would land right next to us as we were praying; flocks of doves would swoop by during our worship time; dust devils would race across my back yard almost dancing the proclamation of God's power. We would laugh hysterically then weep. God would reveal prophetic pictures of things we were supposed to do, and we ran out and did them. We were like two ten year old boys who had had too much Halloween candy. We didn't only see God's glory in nature during this time, we also saw signs of the influence of evil in this world. This was an exciting, eye-opening time for the both of us we will never forget.

The only problem was that I have a wife and we were driving her crazy with our craziness. So, one day during our revival period, when we were jumping out of our skin, we felt compelled to take a sunset drive through the newly built neighborhoods in what had once been orange groves. It was around Halloween time, and as we drove around and prayed, the Spirit was heavy, and we knew God was moving to change the atmosphere everywhere we drove. As we passed a Halloween party in one of the neighborhoods, we saw teenagers dressed up for a party. I remember seeing one young lady with horns that looked so real, I questioned whether I was seeing a costume or not. We were now on guard. All of a sudden something white appeared in the head lights and I screeched to a halt. It was a poodlesque dog, almost shining in the darkness of the moonless night. But this was not any poodle. There was something weird about the way it walked across the street. It was like a crab, shimmying across sideways as it stared directly into our eyes. It didn't really hit us until we parked back in my driveway and Fred said - "Did you see what I just saw?" to which I replied "You mean the sideways walking dog!" to which he replied "Yup."

To this day, I don't know why we saw the dog that day. Was it a sign of the presence of evil in the area - but with a reminder that Satan's attempt at power is almost laughable if we understand the true power of God? I'm not really sure. All I know is that I don't question the works of God. The crazier they are, the more I know it's Him at work because it doesn't make sense otherwise. We live in a physical world, but the Bible clearly describes this as secondary to the spiritual world in which we will live for eternity. When we remind each other of that day, it reminds us that God wants to sometimes invade our physical world with a view of the Kingdom to empower us and to get us excited about what's to come. Fred is that reminder to me - a walking testimony of the crazy love and power of our Father.

♦4♦

Wally World

My dad never taught me how to work on an engine - let alone change a tire. I never learned how to fish or hunt. I never learned how to fix a toaster, or a lamp, or a dishwasher. I never learned about fast cars, or boats. I not only never went to a baseball game with my dad, I never even threw a ball with him. But what my dad lacked in the things that the world says a dad should be, he overflowed in his unique giftedness as a father. My dad lived the serendipitous life. Things would just happen "randomly" to us as a family because my dad not only believed that God was always there watching over him, but he stepped out and did adventurous things just waiting to see what God would do next. My dad lives the abundant life we are all called to in John 10:10 and it was (and still is) infectious. My dad not only stopped to smell the roses, he stopped to lick the rock, to sniff the tree, to shut his eyes and listen to the birds, and to feel the chill of the water as it rushed in the stream. My dad lives life as an adventure that is unfolding every day. He's over 80 now, and he can't stop having fun. My siblings try to slow him down, but he told me recently, "How can I rest when there are so many amazing things to see, so many people in need, and so many friends to hang out with!"

My dad was the only son of a Texas family. His birth certificate says his name is Claren Wallace Collier as he was named after his dad Claren Wady Collier (thank God for the middle name change), but was always Wally. His dad worked for Borden Ice Cream and loved to fish. He was a quietly devout man who just lived life without a lot of fanfare. His wife Bessie was another matter. She was flamboyant and outgoing, a gifted artist who sought out the Holy Spirit in a church upbringing that believed that this part of the Trinity was in hibernation. Somehow this quiet, slightly chubby, bald man found this eccentric loud artist and they found joy and fulfillment in a way that has carried down generationally to their three children who were all involved in marriage ministry, and now down to their grandchildren, and great grandchildren. After my Aunt Flossie was born, my grandmother ("Granny") was told not to have any more children due to the difficulties she had in childbirth. However, my dad was coming into this world one way or another. Granny once pulled my mom aside when she was dating my dad and in a moment of "tmi" told her, "You know, Wally was a child of passion!" as she went on to describe how my gentle granddad "took" my grandma so passionately in a barn one afternoon that he split his condom wide open. Yes, my dad not only broke through into a world that needed more men like him, he came into life with explosive passion which he lives out even today.

But it's not easy being different. My dad wasn't masculine like the other Texas boys. In fact, he not only liked to cook with his mom, but he liked to play with dolls, as his greatest ambition in life was to "be a daddy" someday. What made matters worse was that he was painfully thin and awkward and became an artist like his mother. He was teased mercilessly all through his young adulthood for being a "pansy." But somehow my dad was shielded from the taunts of the world and found his security in Jesus. He leaned so heavily on his heavenly Father that they became one - a power team that has overcome the world with all of its labels and judgments. Like me, Wally went to Abilene Christian University where he fell more in love with art, found the love of his life in my mom Marian, and moved to Nashville, Tennessee with their first son Steve to be with his in-laws and to get his Masters of Art in painting at Peabody College.

When the call went out from his cousin's husband Dwayne who was a minister in the church of Christ (small "c" because it was never meant to be a denomination at its origin), my spontaneous adventurous dad said yes without a lot of deliberation. The "call" was a move by a group of (primarily) teachers and their families to migrate to Long Island, New York (which was almost exclusively Jewish and Catholic and the fastest growing region in the country at that time of the early 60's) to help with a missions effort at the upcoming World's Fair. The Fair (whose monuments still stand today and were immortalized in the movie "Men in Black") was to be held in New York City in 1964 (the year I was born), and what came to be known as "Exodus Bay Shore" had the ultimate goal of planting a church of Christ on Long Island. So, my "very" Southern parents from Houston, Texas and Nashville, Tennessee were now Long Islanders. Although my dad has not lost his Texas twang in all these years, he has surely found the joy, acceptance and love of diversity that is found in all the beautiful Catholic Christians and Jewish lovers of God that he has done life with for all these years.

It wasn't easy working on Long Island as a nerdy High School ceramics teacher with a strong Southern accent who got all the kids they didn't know what to do with. He was teased. He was bullied. But he still loved those broken and lost kids who made fun of him. He started (against all odds) the "God Squad" for anyone at the school who wanted to know about Jesus and spent extra time after school with anyone who needed a shoulder to cry on or someone to pray over them. Amazingly, some of the worst kids who tormented him during his teaching days sought him ought when they became dads and husbands themselves. Those seeds of acceptance and love were planted even though he didn't see the fruit until sometimes 20 years later. He is still planting today as he teaches adult education ceramics to men and women who are trying to find an outlet from the stresses of this world, or shares his passion and love of God at his poetry and memoir classes, or meets with hurting and lonely veterans who long for Wally's big smile and all his stories.

I think all of the four children in our family got a piece of dad - my older brother's nurturing comfort, my sisters passion for the Lord, my younger brother's giftedness in art and love of nature. I'm not sure the biggest thing I got from my dad, but I know all the little things that make up the best parts of me. That ability to be a kid at age 30 - 40 - 50 or even 80. The drive to get up early in the morning to spend time with God - <u>and</u> to get cracking on baking bread, or making muffins or jam - long before anyone else gets up. The heart to reach out to men who've lost their way as husbands or fathers or children of God. The person who has time for people – who doesn't miss the chance to minister to someone at the market or gas station just because they may be late to a church meeting.

My dad is far from perfect, but he is a model of what I believe God is calling men to be. Passionate livers of life. Passionate lovers of their Heavenly Daddy. Passionate husbands, dads and friends. Men who catch the bug and can't go back. Men who are the aroma of Christ. I don't know how long my dad has to still be with us, but I don't think God will open the doors to heaven until they are well rested and ready to get moving because Wally is coming!

♦ 5 ♦

4,992 and Counting

I've been married for 32 years and have one of the happiest and most fulfilling marriages that I know, but it's a battle. Because a happy marriage is the foundation for raising kids well, for bearing fruit in ministry, and also for a well balanced work life, it is a major target for Satan to attack. Marriages are fruitful ground for the enemy because despite the physical attraction that draws the two sexes together in a perfect connection, women and men are so different in the way they think, feel and react that conflict is inevitable. If not tended to properly (more later), this conflict can lead to resentment, disconnection and ultimately either apathy or bitterness. Satan has already won ground in this area by convincing society that divorce is not only acceptable, but a good option when things are not going well, needs are not being met, or feelings have faded. This landed in our backyard about 10 years ago when the first of a number of our friends' marriages crashed after 20 years together. These were not just any friends, these were strong Christians in ministry who (on the surface) appeared to have everything together. But something was wrong.

So, if Satan is out to kill and destroy marriages, how do we fight back not only in our marriages, but in supporting our friends and family? Well, after seeing these marriages dissolve seemingly out of the blue, we began talking to divorced friends who were willing to tell their story. We also began hanging out with young couples (particularly those working in ministry) to see what was going on in early marriage that might be laying a bad foundation that couldn't last the test of time. One of the interesting things we found out from divorced women was that they caught their husbands having a real or emotional affair because the husbands were writing love notes, giving gifts and going on romantic dates with another woman - the exact behavior they should have been doing with their wives in order to build a healthy marriage. The men who had the affairs mentioned that the women they connected with were really interested in them, encouraged and built them up and were very responsive sexually - the exact behavior that wives should have been exhibiting with their husbands in order to build a healthy marriage.

This isn't rocket science, but Satan has made it seem like the impossible. In order to have a healthy, happy and affair-proof marriage, the man needs to treat his wife like he did when they were dating – that is, romance her, write her notes, give her gifts, take her on dates, spend time talking and (especially) listening to her. In my experience in not only my own marriage, but in the couples we mentor and our close couple friends, if the husband continues to "date" his wife, all things that men generally complain about in marriage - lack of sex, disrespect, and nagging - seem to magically disappear over time. In particular, if a man romances his wife, the natural and God-ordained result of emotional intimacy between a husband and wife will be sexual intimacy. But the sexual is really hard to get to without work at the emotional part.

On the other side, men are pretty simple creatures. If a wife will encourage (i.e., be her husband's biggest fan and tell him how much she appreciates and is proud of him), be interested (even if slightly feigned) in his work or hobbies or sports, and be responsive sexually on a regular basis, men will respond in an amazing way. In our experience, even if the husband is not naturally romantic, he will be very open to working on it if these other things are in place.

The problem is that couples tend to fall into the rut of focusing on the other spouse's behavior rather than their own. So, it is very common to hear a wife tell us that she is unresponsive sexually because the husband is rude or harsh or not hearing her heart. It is also very common for a husband to tell us that he is not motivated to romance his wife because she is naggy or bitchy to him, doesn't appreciate all he does for the family and is a cold fish in the bedroom.

My wife and I were blessed by being raised by parents who not only had excellent, happy and healthy marriages, but were also in marriage ministry - Libby's through the church and mine through the great program out the Catholic Church - Marriage Encounter. In watching both of our parents live life as a couple and being exposed to some good marriage books (my favorite being *Every Man's*

Marriage by Steve Arterburn), we quickly learned some "tricks" to having the abundant marriage we both wanted, but is often so elusive to most couples. First, we learned that we needed to set aside time every day to connect to one another. This is something that happens during the dating relationship, but is often lost after the wedding day. We were once on a question and answer panel with couple friends of ours who minister at a large church and have a lot of people tugging for their time. Someone asked about having a "date night" which is something a lot of healthy couples do to make sure they connect every week. The wife's response was interesting. She said that "the worst advice she and her husband got during pre-marriage counseling was to make sure to have a date night once a week." After the audience gasped in confusion, she explained herself. "It's great to have a date night once a week - but that's not enough - if you aren't connecting emotionally during the week, then date night generally turns into 'fight night' because not only are there a number of unresolved issues to be dealt with, but because you have not connected as a couple, the 'dealing' is often done in a caustic, blaming or griping way. On the other hand, if a couple has stayed connected during the week, the special 'date night' can just be fun, romantic and bonding."

With the need of daily connection in mind, Libby and I started something in early marriage that takes work, but has lasted through busy work and ministry schedules, twins, four kids under five years old, teenagers, and a very active social life. We call it "every night is date night" meaning we make an effort every night possible (that means we do it unless one of us is out of town and then do it over the phone) to make an appointment to connect. It's fun if this can be done out at a restaurant or a coffee shop, but that's not always possible with kids or money issues, so we just set up a home date. That means setting a time and location to meet (perhaps after the kids are down or after the football game), taking turns preparing for the date (e.g., preparing food and/or drinks or just cleaning up an area and lighting a candle and turning on music), and - most importantly - coming prepared. That means taking a shower or bath, putting on clothes as if you were still dating (i.e., no saggy sweats for women or frumpy shorts and undershirt for men) and doing whatever it takes to let go of the stress of the day.

Then be ready to love on your spouse. If you've never done this before, it is surprisingly hard at first. Wives get frustrated that the husband doesn't listen well, husbands get impatient and bored, there are interruptions from smart phones or needy children, and nagging and bickering start rearing their ugly head. But hang on! If you stay invested, this time will be like it is for us - something we look forward to every night, something we now couldn't live without, and something that keeps our marriage not only affair proof, but happy and fulfilling.

One of the reasons date night every night works so well is that it is God's plan for us to connect as couples both emotionally and physically. He created us as two very distinct beings made to not only be attracted to the ways we are different, but to have our bodies perfectly connect to one another's. If you are married you know that sex not only bonds us physically, but also emotionally. It is a crucial part of marriage. If it is failing or non-existent, it is not only a sign of problems in a marriage, it leaves a marriage at great risk for failure as one of the spouses (usually the man) will stray either emotionally or physically through porn or an affair. It's an amazing thing, but when you actually practice date night every night, not only will you be more connected as a couple, fight less, and have more fun together, it is only natural that your sex life will be better and more consistent. The main reason for this is that when a woman is receiving emotional intimacy from her husband through romance and a listening ear, her God created response is to respond sexually. This is the great circle of an abundant marriage. Emotional intimacy leads to sexual intimacy which deepens emotional intimacy and so on. Although it takes time to build momentum in this area, and a couple can fall into ruts at times, if you truly work at it and make it a priority, this abundant marriage circle is very powerful and can lead to the marriage both the husband and wife have always dreamed of.

Libby and I had the great blessing of being able to live with our best friends for a nine month season when their family was in a season between the secular working world and full-time ministry. Both of us had very happy marriages and both made the effort to connect with each other on a daily basis in order to maintain intimacy, both emotionally and sexually. This was not only an extremely fun time for us and our children, but also very educational as we watched another couple interact on a daily basis mostly in healthy, but often unhealthy ways as well. One thing the husbands began to notice was that when the other was overly critical, grumpy, dismissive, used cutting humor or was crude around his wife, the wife would shut down emotionally. Even if they ultimately had "date" time, the damage done from even one "bad" moment from the husband meant that emotional and especially sexual intimacy were out the window. On the other hand, if the husband was loving, gentle, helpful or romantic, it was amazing how the wife responded in the direction toward intimacy.

In order to help each other in this area, we developed what we called "GFP" or "BFP" to label things we did during the day. If my friend did (or was planning to do) something that would be a deterrent to intimacy, I told him that was "BFP" or "bad foreplay." If it was something to promote intimacy, it was "GFP" or "good foreplay." Although this sounds crude or too focused on sex, recall the main reason for affairs - husbands stray because of a lack of physical intimacy and wives tend to stray due to a lack of emotional intimacy. Accept it or not, this became a great tool for my buddy and I in our marriages because if we actually thought about our behavior in terms of whether it would lead to intimacy or not, this was a great motivator. I hear a lot of women complain that their husbands are ONLY romantic and spend date time with them, or are nice, when they want sex. Why, they ask, can't they just be a good husband without expecting a sexual response. I ask the opposite question, "Why is this bad?" God gave men a strong sex drive and physical attraction to women to promote the Biblical concept of marriage and family.

Although modern society and pornography have made sex an "act" which is disassociated from emotional connection, God created sex to be a beautiful, fun and bonding way for couples to connect which is not only the natural after-effect to emotional intimacy, but something that makes it even stronger. Our wives got this concept and our marriages became more abundant because of it. They even started using GFP and BFP for their behavior as well, because they wanted to do everything in their power during the day to work toward an intimate night with their husbands.

Well, after over 30 years of marriage, our plan has worked. We are happier, more fulfilled, more understood, and have better sex every year we are married. It just keeps getting better. I once met a man who had been married for 60 years and as we were visiting I told him I was about to celebrate my 25th anniversary. His response was "Wow, I'm so excited for you because the 2nd 25 are so much better than the first." This is counter-cultural in an age when couples don't only "try-out" marriage before committing and therefore get married later in life, but also give up after seven years, or more commonly after 20 years when the kids leave the house and there is nothing left to bond them together because they spent little if any time creating intimacy that would last.

I have a friend who is a deacon in the Catholic Church. As he goes around the country on missions to build up marriages and people's relationship with God, he explains why people do things that are counter to God's instructions in the Bible. His theory is that although people go to church and talk the talk, they don't REALLY believe that God's way is better. They therefore fall back on their own intelligence, common sense and what society says is the way to a better life. This leads to disappointment, depression and divorce. I am here to say that God's way is better particularly when it comes to marriage. I dare any single person to match up with me (a guy who only dated one girl, was a virgin when I got married, never had an affair, and has been married for over 30 years) in my fulfillment AND consistency in the sexual arena. It is a lie when society tells us that good and frequent sex ends on the wedding day. When you begin to do it God's way (even after mistakes in the past), and actually work at it, not only your overall marriage, but your sex life will be what God made it to be - AMAZING!

So, after reading this chapter you may have finally figured out the title - "4,992 and Counting." Since I got married, although it fluctuates during different seasons of life, including pregnancy/baby time when sex is less frequent by nature vs. vacation time when it can be every day, I can honestly say that my wife and I have sex at least 3 times per week on average.

Based upon the "Every Man's Battle" theory of a 72 hour cycle for men's sperm reproduction and the results of trying to have "Date Night Every Night," this is just about right. So, if I do the math – 52 weeks a year times 3 times 32 years, I get the whopping number of 4,992 as of December, 2017 - impressive, but only the beginning.

♦ 6 ♦

"Why are you talking about having no bread?"

We all know the story of Jesus feeding the 4,000 (which was really more like 15,000 as the number only included men) with only seven loaves of bread and a few small fish, but it's what happens right after that miracle which I believe is so impactful on how to live a Kingdom centered life.

The story, from Mark chapter 8, verse 14, begins with Jesus and the disciples getting into a boat to cross to the other side of the Sea of Galilee from the region of the Decapolis. Mark reflects that the disciples had forgotten to bring bread except for one loaf - which was interesting in that there were seven basketfuls of breadcrumbs left over after the feeding of the 4,000. Jesus, somehow discerning their anxiety, warns, "Be careful. Watch out for the yeast of the Pharisees and that of Herod." The perplexed disciples then discus this warning and conclude, "It is because we have no bread."

Jesus' response to the disciples' anxiety is at the heart of why it is so hard to gain total freedom from the shackles of the world.

> "'Why are you talking about having no bread? Do you not see or understand? Are your hearts hardened? Do you have eyes but fail to see, and ears but fail to hear? And don't you remember? When I broke the five loaves for the five thousand, how many basketfuls of pieces did you pick up?' 'Twelve,' they replied. 'And when I broke the seven loaves for the four thousand, how many basketfuls of pieces did you pick up?' They answered, 'Seven,' He said to them 'Do you still not understand.'"

The disciples had the same problem we do today in America. God blesses us richly. He sends the money right at the last minute to meet our needs. Our children are not only ALWAYS fed, but have more than any children in the world. The longer we live, the more times we see God's hand enter into a situation and miraculously provide, or heal, or save. Yet, as soon as the miracle happens, we forget. We forget that what was so impossible has actually happened. That God has done it again and brought the Kingdom to earth. Instead of saying in the midst of the "next" crisis that, "surely God will provide in His own way and in His own time, so I will not worry," we freak out, complain, get anxious, lose our faith, and live in misery until He comes through yet again. Not exactly as we ask, but always in a way that is better for us.

Why do we do this? Why do we suffer for no reason? Why do we doubt after seeing miracle after miracle? I believe the reason lies in the fact that we don't really believe that God's way is the better way. We talk the talk of faith, but when push comes to shove, we would rather rely on our own strength, or in the security of the yeast of the world (Herod) or religion (The Pharisees), than in the seeming uncertainty involved in living by the Spirit.

This concept is seen in a striking way in Numbers 11 after the Israelites had been wandering in the desert a short time after being delivered from Egypt. God had been providing manna every morning for His people, but they wanted more. "Manna" in Hebrew literally means "What is it?" It appeared with the dew in the morning like frost on the ground. It was "white like coriander seed, and it tasted like honey wafers." (Exodus 16:31 NLT) I believe this was God's way of telling His children that they were not going to understand His provision, but if they would only trust Him, it would not only be there every day, but would be sweet and special and so good for them. Now remember our nature as humans to worry. The loving Father fixed this by not allowing His children to store the manna but for the day before the Sabbath. If they did, it would rot and become infested with maggots. They had to just trust God's provision every day. And you know what - it was ALWAYS there for them.

But, in what we should all feel is all too familiar to how we relate to God, the sweet provision of our Father was not enough.

> "And the people of Israel also began to complain. 'Oh, for some meat!' they exclaimed. 'We remember the fish we used to eat for free in Egypt. And we had all the cucumbers, melons, leeks, onions, and garlic we wanted. But now our appetites are gone. All we ever see is this manna! ... Oh, for some meat! We were better off in Egypt!'" (Numbers 11:4b-18 NLT)

Well, as the Father will do, when His children whine and whine about what they don't have rather than rejoicing in what He has provided to them, He finally tells Moses that He will give them what they want and they "will have to eat it. And it won't be for just a day or two, or for five or ten or even twenty. You will eat it for a whole month until you gag and are sick of it." Oh the misery we ask for. Numbers 11:31- 34 reports what happens next.

> "Now the Lord sent a wind that brought quail from the sea and let them fall all around the camp. For miles in every direction there were quail flying about three feet off the ground. So the people went out and caught quail all that day and throughout the night and all the next day, too. No one gathered less than fifty bushels! They spread the quail all around the camp to dry. But while they were gorging themselves on the meat - while it was still in their mouths - the anger of the Lord blazed against the people, and He struck them with a severe plague. So that place was called

> Kibroth-hattavah (which means 'graves of gluttony') because there they buried the people who had craved meat from Egypt."

Isn't this so like us. God provides for our needs every day. He provides evidence that He is with us every day - not exactly like the cloud the Israelites had - but in that chance encounter, that serendipitous event, that "random" check in the mail. We are free because He set us free. But we forget. We get comfortable and safe and the enemy starts to whisper things in our ear and we listen. Now, God's daily provision is not enough. We want what we used to have or what our neighbors have or what the world tells us satisfies.

In whining for what they had in Egypt, the people were actually longing for the meat of their own captivity. If we are honest, we are no different. We aren't satisfied with the "uncertainty" of God's daily provision. We want a savings account. We want a guaranteed salary. We want vacation time. We want escape. We want a pre-nuptial agreement with God that says, "We love you and want to be with you, but don't ever steal our stuff!" We know that living with reliance on the things of the world, like Egypt, is slavery to us, but we still want it. What better evidence that Satan has established strongholds among God's people than that despite our miraculous freedom and His impossible provision, the lust for the things of the world overcomes us and we blindly chase after the things that will only work to bind us yet again into a place of slavery – our own personal Kibroth-hattavah - only to force us to wake up, repent, and ask our loving Father to save us yet again.

God wants to call this generation to a new pathway. A pathway carved in full reliance on the Father. This is Kingdom living. The amazing thing is that when we fully rely on God, He somehow not only gives us back all we were chasing after, but gives it back to us in a pure way that is all Him and none of us. When we attain it on our own, we can't help ourselves but to become overwhelmed with worry and anxiety in our attempt to guard it. However, when all we have comes from God, our hands open up – we become givers - we wake up every morning in expectancy of what He will do that day - we walk in freedom and not in bondage. This is the abundant life! Now go live it!

♦ 7 ♦

Is it God or is it Satan?

If you ever come and visit my house someday to pray or hang out on my back porch, you will experience something truly special and a gift from God. When we bought our house out in the country in Riverside County, California back in 1999, it was dirt with some pepper and fruit trees scattered over a little over an acre of land and a house up on a hill overlooking the lower part of the property. The special part was that there was a small stream running through the lower property coming out of what was then the orange groves, across the street through our property, and out to our neighbors yard and beyond. As the yard took shape piece by piece that first year, one thing we did was grab our neighbor (who had a Bobcat) and have him dig a pond for us - what a joy and what a hassle (only pond owners will get this) that pond has been over the years.

One of the joys (and curses) of the pond has been the vast array of ducks who come to visit our backyard during the winter, and the pet ducks who have been part of the family over the years - from Doc and Mr. Bill in the early days, to wonderful and quirky George the Afro-Duck (look it up) who was a loner with us for over 7 years, to Quackers and Beakers (2 beautiful white Peking ducks that a young boy from our neighborhood asked to live with us after becoming too big for his baby pool). The problem with Quackers is that he was "the man" and didn't like having George around with his wife or in his new home at all. The other problem is the fact about ducks you probably didn't know (apart from them having corkscrew shaped penises) - they are the only species other than man that rapes - yes, dark and weird and troubling, but very true.

Well, when Quackers hit the scene, not only did he rape his wife (which includes biting the back of her neck and dunking her head under the water as he mounts her almost to the point of drowning – sorry), but he raped George every day to the point of him being bloodied and broken. After numerous attempts by my kids to intervene and pleading by my daughter Becky to please kill Quackers, God (or Satan) worked it out. After a weekend away with my wife Libby, I came home to find George missing. This wasn't unusual during the recent "Shawshank Redemption" period of his life where he would find places to hide away from the rapist, but when I went out the next morning and he was gone, I knew something was amiss. I then noticed that the other two ducks were missing as well. As I walked around the pond in search, I heard a meek high pitched squeak from under our bridge. It was Beakers, literally covered in duck blood from the slaughter of her beloved (yet abusive) husband who supposedly suffered the same fate as George - a racoon got him.

I am getting somewhere with this story although it is a giant rabbit trail. At this point in the story, Beakers is all alone having had her husband murdered so close to her she was covered in his blood (Satan), but she was now free from his abuse (God), but our beloved George had also been murdered (Satan), but he was now free from his suffering after a long and happy life (God). Then, within a week of the "Great Duck Massacre on Owl Tree Road" I got a text from one of my wife's friends as follows: "MY NEIGHBOR HAS A BLACK DUCK WHO IS TORMENTING HER TURKEYS – CAN HE MOVE TO YOUR POND?" The answer was a quick yes, and when we got home that night, we had a beautiful mixed race black duck with a green head and (yes, believe it), an "S" emblazoned on his chest in white. My son and I named him Clark and what a joy he has been. He and Beakers (renamed Lois) quickly fell in love, became inseparable, and even their duck mating was sweet and calm (although still screwy). As I sat on a bench near the pond the morning I was about to write this chapter, the black and white duck just hung out with me, enjoying life and each other in this little paradise God has blessed me with.

I didn't plan this duck story which had ended so well. I would have never prayed for it because I loved George and never wanted to lose him. I didn't pray for Quakers to be murdered - although I'm pretty sure my daughter did. I haven't had a critter kill a cat or duck in my property for over 10 years since we have fenced it all in. Yet, it happened. Was it God's plan? Was it Satan's? Did God allow Quackers and George to die so that he could redeem things through Clark? My answer - it doesn't matter! I felt like God was telling me through the ducks that it's not always black and white - sometimes the black or white, the God or Satan, the good or bad are just part of our story of life in the Kingdom of God.

"And we know that in all things God works for the good of those who love him, who have been called according to his purpose." (Roman 8:28 NIV) This scripture comes directly after Paul tells us how the Spirit helps us in our weakness, and is followed directly by Paul telling us that God "foreknew" us and "predestined" us not in that he is the cause of everything that goes on, but in order "to be conformed to the image of his Son." That is, God works everything (whether seemingly good or seemingly bad) in our lives "for the good" as part of his eternal purpose of "conforming" us to the "image" of Jesus who died the ugliest and most painful of deaths so that the human race could be redeemed and live eternally.

We spend way too much energy (me being the main culprit) trying to understand whether God caused something or Satan caused something or God allowed something to happened or God allowed Satan to cause something to happen. All of these can be backed up by scripture, but I think dwelling on them too much either for ourselves or others, leads to confusion, anger, pride and sometimes depression, when we just don't understand at the time why we lost our job, or our spouse or our child, or we get cancer. The bottom line is that in our greatest triumphs in life AND in our greatest tragedies God is there and he will "conform us" through the process.

This concept is beautifully illustrated in an allegory shared by beloved author Max Lucado that he learned from his Portugese instructor when he was a missionary in Brazil.

> "Once there was an old man who lived in a tiny village. Although poor, he was envied by all, for he owned a beautiful white horse. Even the king coveted his treasure. A horse like this had never been seen before - such was its splendor, its majesty, its strength.
>
> People offered fabulous prices for the steed, but the old man always refused. 'This horse is not a horse to me,' he would tell them. 'It is a person. How could you sell a person? He is a friend, not a possession. How could you sell a friend?' The man was poor and the temptation was great. But he never sold the horse.
>
> One morning he found that the horse was not in the stable. All the village came to see him. 'You old fool,' they scoffed, 'we told you that someone would steal your horse. We warned you that you would be robbed. You are so poor. How could you ever hope to protect such a valuable animal? It would have been better to have sold him. You could have gotten whatever price you wanted. No amount would have been too high. Now the horse is gone, and you've been cursed with misfortune.'
>
> The old man responded, 'Don't speak too quickly. Say only that the horse is not in the stable. That is all we know; the rest is judgment. If I've been cursed or not, how can you know? How can you judge?'
>
> The people contested, 'Don't make us out to be fools! We may not be philosophers, but great philosophy is not needed. The simple fact that your horse is gone is a curse.'

The old man spoke again. ‘All I know is that the stable is empty, and the horse is gone. The rest I don’t know. Whether it be a curse or a blessing, I can’t say. All we can see is a fragment. Who can say what will come next?’

The people of the village laughed. They thought that the man was crazy. They had always thought he was fool; if he wasn’t, he would have sold the horse and lived off the money. But instead, he was a poor woodcutter, an old man still cutting firewood and dragging it out of the forest and selling it. He lived hand to mouth in the misery of poverty. Now he had proven that he was, indeed, a fool.

After fifteen days, the horse returned. He hadn’t been stolen; he had run away into the forest. Not only had he returned, he had brought a dozen wild horses with him. Once again the village people gathered around the woodcutter and spoke. ‘Old man, you were right and we were wrong. What we thought was a curse was a blessing. Please forgive us.’

The man responded, ‘Once again, you go too far. Say only that the horse is back. State only that a dozen horses returned with him, but don’t judge. How do you know if this is a blessing or not? You see only a fragment. Unless you know the whole story, how can you judge? You read only one page of a book. Can you judge the whole book? You read only one word of a phrase. Can you understand the entire phrase? Life is so vast, yet you judge all of life with one page or one word. All you have is a fragment! Don’t say that this is a blessing. No one knows. I am content with what I know. I am not perturbed by what I don’t.’

‘Maybe the old man is right,’ they said to one another. So they said little. But down deep, they knew he was wrong. They knew it was a blessing. Twelve wild horses had returned with one horse. With a little bit of work, the animals could be broken and trained and sold for much money.

The old man had a son, an only son. The young man began to break the wild horses. After a few days, he fell from one of the horses and broke both legs. Once again the villagers gathered around the old man and cast their judgments.

'You were right,' they said. 'You proved you were right. The dozen horses were not a blessing. They were a curse. Your only son has broken his legs, and now in your old age you have no one to help you. Now you are poorer than ever.'

The old man spoke again. 'You people are obsessed with judging. Don't go so far. Say only that my son broke his legs. Who knows if it is a blessing or a curse? No one knows. We only have a fragment. Life comes in fragments.'

It so happened that a few weeks later the country engaged in war against a neighboring country. All the young men of the village were required to join the army. Only the son of the old man was excluded, because he was injured. Once again the people gathered around the old man, crying and screaming because their sons had been taken. There was little chance that they would return. The enemy was strong, and the war would be a losing struggle. They would never see their sons again.

'You were right, old man,' they wept. 'God knows you were right. This proves it. Yours son's accident was a blessing. His legs may be broken, but at least he is with you. Our sons are gone forever.'

> The old man spoke again. 'It is impossible to talk with you. You always draw conclusions. No one knows. Say only this: Your sons had to go to war, and mine did not. No one knows if it is a blessing or a curse. No one is wise enough to know. Only God knows.'
>
> The old man was right. We only have a fragment. Life's mishaps and horrors are only a page out of a grand book. We must be slow about drawing conclusions. We must reserve judgment on life's storms until we know the whole story."
>
> (*The Woodcutter's Wisdom and Other Favorite Stories*, Word Publishing 1995, Max Lucado)

One of the main reasons I battled anxiety which then led to depression, even though my life to the outside world seemed idyllic, was that when a situation arose in my life that was troubling I would go to catastrophic thinking about it. I would tell myself things (i.e., lies) like "You're a fake and everyone is going to find you out", or "You're going to lose everything," or "You can never leave your job because that's all you know how to do." Satan is a professional at feasting on our fears and insecurities and tempting us to take them to their worst case scenarios to basically take us out of the game. That's what he did to me. But he didn't win and he won't win with you.

When I crashed and hit rock bottom with severe and crippling anxiety and depression, I knew this wasn't me, but I couldn't dig my way out. I prayed, I got prayer, I ate better, I exercised, I tried taking drugs, but nothing worked. I just knew that the thing that happened to me would cause everything I had worked so hard to accomplish - my family, my home, my career, my relationships - to crash and burn. This was a huge lie from Satan, but I had bought in on it.

When I was beginning to lose hope that I would ever become myself again (which is a scary place to be), my wife pulled a Hail Mary. She researched the best place to go if you are suffering from anxiety and depression and found a place in Edmonds, Washington called "The Center – A Place of HOPE", run by the amazing Dr. Gregg Jantz. As we were facing a financial crises, the huge (but worth it) cost of The Center just made me more anxious. Well, as He usually does, God showed up in an amazing way through our friend Rob. During a time of prayer he asked my wife if she would allow him to reach out to our friends who loved us so much, and we had invested so much in over the years, be totally open about my situation and ask for help. The result is a testimony to trusting God and getting beyond the fact that you are embarrassed or guilty or ashamed and letting the Body of Christ do what it was designed to do. It's a long story of testimonies, but in 3 days, my friends and family donated $25,000 toward my healing, a lot of the money coming from those who (in human terms) couldn't afford it – like missionaries we had previously supported and were now supporting us.

To be honest, as much as the The Center was a major piece in my ultimate full and complete recovery, my time in Edmonds was horrible - it was cold and rainy and miserable for a Southern Californian like myself. I was so anxious I couldn't play sports at the free gym they supplied, my head was so foggy, I couldn't read the awesome books they gave us, and I was so depressed that all I wanted to do was sleep which I did a lot. However, I met and became friends with some wonderful, loving and inspirational people from all over the country who were battling the same demons I was - and overcoming them while loving and accepting me for where I was in the journey. Plus, I went to class every day, day in and day out and listened. I didn't realize it at the time, but while I "believed" the concepts of healing they were teaching me weren't soaking in, they were. God was doing a mighty work in me through them.

Of all the things I learned at The Center that have stuck with me as I now walk in freedom, the one that was most crucial to not only my healing, but my continuing healthy and victorious journey, is the concept of "Radical Acceptance." In a nutshell, radical acceptance means that whatever comes your way in life, whether seemingly or obviously bad, you just accept it, even if that acceptance seems radical. It doesn't mean you like it, or label it - you just accept it, know God is still there with you conforming you into His image, and move on with life. This acceptance is complete and total - from the depths of your soul. The alternative is to dwell on it, ruminate about it, and live in misery. The "bad" event is still there, but now you've added misery to it which leads to anxiety and depression and beyond. Radical acceptance is the way to turn suffering that can't be tolerated into pain that can.

Life will throw you curveballs - sometimes it will even throw at your head (and hit it) - but if we can learn from the woodcutter and remind ourselves that we don't know the full story yet, and that God is right there with us to make "all things work together for good", life is still full of challenges, but we become overcomers rather than victims of them. That's why people can say crazy things like cancer, or jail, or losing my job was "the best thing that ever happened to me" - because God is not only a redeeming God, He's a radical God!

♦ 8 ♦

"And the angel of the Lord said unto him, Wherefore hast thou smitten thine ass these three times?"

Have you ever felt like you heard from God and set out on a path, only to have it blocked? This happened in the physical to me recently and I really believe God was using it as a metaphor for a spiritual lesson he was trying to teach me.

My wife and I headed out on a week long road trip one early morning with a plan and a path in mind. We were heading up to Northern California to visit our dear friends who had moved to Redding, and then planned on driving back along the famous Pacific Coast Highway to see the beautiful sights, but also to have some much needed bonding time together. One of the main reasons I wanted to go to Redding was not only to visit with our friends who had had a tough year, but to also talk with my friend about the potential of a business partnership. He had always been a "go to" guy for me in business and was someone I could rely upon to give me wise and experienced counsel, particularly for a person like me who was insecure about my business savvy. I was beginning a new chapter in life and felt like God had destined my friend and I to connect in business as this would give me the security and confidence I was lacking in myself. This made sense as we both had recently escaped the "rat race" of being big firm litigators and also had been talking about working together since the time we were in law school over 25 years ago. It was God's plan.

As we headed off on our journey, our route was set to go North on the 15 Freeway and then cut over on the 58 to head toward our first night's location in Paso Robles. The problem began when I noticed a huge "X" on my navigation system right on the 58 freeway. After tuning on to news radio, we learned that the recent rains in the Southern California mountains (after years of drought) had caused some mudslides which completely blocked the freeway. So, our path was rerouted across to Valencia to head up the 5 freeway (known as the Grapevine) to continue on our journey. However, we soon learned that the mudslides had also hit the Grapevine in a huge way not only blocking the freeway in both directions but trapping people in their cars. Our second way blocked, we decided to make the best of it and drive further west and go through beautiful Santa Barbara where two of our daughters live. We could have lunch with our daughter who had been going through some friend issues and needed to talk, and then proceed to Paso Robles a bit later, foregoing some of our wine tasting plans.

Well, as we listened to the news, the traffic reporters were telling all of Southern California that the ONLY way up to Northern California was to go through Santa Barbara and then to Paso Robles - the exact way we were going. That meant that not only every car headed north was going the same way, but every truck which normally went another route, was now passing through Santa Barbara and Paso Robles. We did have a great and much needed visit with our daughter, but all in all, the "blocking" turned a 4 hour journey into a 10 hour one.

We headed out early the next morning from Paso Robles with the intention of getting to Redding by lunchtime. Then it happened again. We were headed up the 880 toward the Bay Area and beyond when my navigator showed another huge "X" on the 880 and rerouted us to the 680 - which I had never been on before even having done work in Oakland and San Francisco over the years as a lawyer. It was about 7:00 am, and as my wife came out of her slumber she asked where we were, and I told her that we had been rerouted through Oakland. She then told me her girlfriend who had recently reached out to her for prayer due to a family crisis lived near Oakland in a town called Pleasanton. Believe it or not, as we looked again at our trusted navigator, we were smack dab in the middle of Pleasanton. We ended up going to her house for coffee, some prayer and a big hug, and were then off on our way again after the "blocking" led to another God assignment that blessed not only our friend, but us in a huge way.

It's a long story, but after finally getting to Redding, and having time to sit down with my friend, it became very clear that this was not the time to enter into a business relationship. Not that something won't happen in the future (as it likely will), but "God's plan" for my next step in life was officially blocked, just like the freeways. We had a lovely evening out with our friends, but the next morning I woke up with some feelings I had not experienced for awhile - anxiety and fear about the future. My plan had not worked out - my insurance policy was off the table - I now had some unknowns ahead of me. I needed faith, but was ruminating on "what ifs".

As I started to pray in bed that morning, I distinctly heard God ask me, "Why did I block your path?" If you've never been to Redding before, there is a wonderful and holy place located at Bethel Church where they have set up a 24/7 prayer room to just hang out with God. Since I was up before everyone else, I decided to head to the prayer room and see what God had to say. As I looked back at the events of the day before, I felt like God was trying to teach me a spiritual truth through the physical - that there is ANOTHER way, a way that is not the path of fear or pride or what the world says is the right or safe way. This way is all God and none of me. It has no arrogance, it is true, it is MY path - full of adventure and provision and serendipities and breakthrough.

After writing this down in my journal, I felt like God had a message for me about the blocked path and it was in the story of Balaam and his donkey (or ass if you use the King James version). When I opened up my iPad to read, God's message for me that day became clear as the screen just opened up to the wonderful devotional written by Sarah Young called "Jesus Calling" which has blessed so many people over the last few years. It read as follows:

> "Go gently through this day, keeping your eyes on me. I will open up the way before you as you take steps of trust along your path. Sometimes the way before you appears to be blocked. If you focus on the obstacle or search for a way around it you will probably go off course. Instead focus on me, the Shepherd who is leading you along your life journey. Before you know it, the 'obstacle' will be behind you and you will hardly know how you passed through it. This is the secret of success in my kingdom. Although you remain aware of the visible world around you, your primary awareness is of me. When the road before you looks rocky, you can trust me to get you through that rough patch. My presence enables you to face each day with confidence."

I try to read through the Bible every year using a reading program like the *One Year Bible*. For some reason over the years the story of Balaam has frustrated me, particularly as Balaam is used as an example of being "unrighteous" (2 Peter 2:15) and "ungodly" (Jude 11). My reading of his story has always shown me that although tempted to curse Israel by the Moabites, he listened to God. Although initially told not to go, ended up being allowed by God to travel to Moab where he went on to blessed the Israelites. Yet, God got "angry" at Balaam and blocked his path with his own ass (donkey). Why did God get so mad? Why does Revelation 2:12 chastise the church at Pergamum for tolerating "teaching" that is "like that of Balaam?" When I started to read the story again in light of what had happened, and what God was telling me, it started to make sense for the first time.

You probably know the story from Sunday School, but here's how it goes beginning in Numbers Chapter 22. The Israelites, led by Moses, were still traveling through the wilderness towards the Holy Land when they traveled to the "plains of Moab" which were along the Jordan across from Jericho. Their king, Balak, had heard stories about the Israelites, believed them to be too powerful for his people and decided to do something "spiritual" about it. His spiritual solution was a man named Balaam, who was famous at the time for being a "diviner" or someone who was so in touch with God that he had the power to summon up divine powers. We don't know all that it meant to be a diviner in Balaam's day, but Balaam was clearly in a personal relationship with Jehovah God as Numbers 22:12 says "God came to Balaam", and in verse 18, Balaam declares that the Lord is "my God."

Balak sent a message (as well as a fee) together with leaders from Moab to convince Balaam to curse Israel so that he would be able to defeat them. "For I know that whoever you bless is blessed, and whoever you curse is cursed" - a testimony to the acclaim that Balaam had at the time. Balaam then asks the elders to spend the night so that he can ask the Lord what to do. The next morning Balaam gives them his answer that "The Lord has refused to let me go with you." In fact, God clearly told him that he "must not put a curse on those people, because they are blessed."

However, Balak was determined (through fear) to get his way. He therefore sent a large contingent of "more distinguished" officials to try to convince Balaam. Balaam's response to the second visit is telling as he explains to the officials, "Even if Balak gave me all the silver and gold in his palace, I could not do anything great or small to go beyond the command of the Lord my God." (Numbers 22:18, NIV) What's interesting is that even though Balaam says this and knows God's will is to bless Israel, he still goes back and asks God AGAIN whether God is sure as to what he said the first time.

God's response to Balaam coming back is to say, "Since these men have come to summon you, go with them, but do only what I tell you." (Numbers 22:20, NIV) This reminded me of what I do in my own life to fit "my plans" or "my security" into "God's will." We go to him and say "I know what you said God, but are you really sure I shouldn't do what I want to do." And God (as He will) lets us go down that path. God knows what will ultimately happen and the curse will be turned into a blessing, but it doesn't make him happy. Just like a good parent, God was disappointed with Balaam that he didn't get it and was so influenced by power and money.

Next is the fun part, particularly in the King James version. Numbers 22:21 tells us that,

> "And God's anger was kindled because he went: and the angel of the Lord stood in the way for an adversary against him. Now he was riding upon his ass, and his two servants were with him. And the ass saw the angel of the Lord standing in the way, and his sword drawn in his hand: and the ass turned aside out of the way, and went into the field: and Balaam smote the ass, to turn her into the way."

The angel blocked his path three times, but Balaam was determined to go the way he wanted to go so he kept beating his donkey until finally, his ass spoke. (Back to the NIV) "What have I done to you to make you beat me these three times? … Am I not your own donkey, which you have always ridden, to this day? Have I been in the habit of doing this to you?" Doesn't this sound like God when we fail to follow his path out of insecurity or pride of lust for what the world has to offer?

As I read this passage, it came clearly to me that sometimes I just need to listen to my own ass - that God provided inner voice that comes with a close relationship to God. That voice which, like the donkey was always trustworthy, without ulterior motive - just pure, simple and trusted. But we fight against that voice even though we know - because God has told us clearly in many cases either directly or through His word, what His will is for us. So even when we go down the path that still has a toe in the world, sometimes really believing it to be God's will because we have convinced ourselves of such (and God may have consented due to our stubbornness), and then when that path doesn't go as we thought or it is blocked, we push on with our own strength (now driven by fear or anger) and go against everything we know to be true until God finally reveals himself like he did through the angel with Balaam. In Balaam's case, the angel revealed that even though he was fighting his trusted donkey (that inner voice screaming for us to stop), that thing he was beating actually saved his life as the angel was set to kill him. In Balaam's case, I believe he was not only motivated to go by his pride from the influential people seeking him out and the money involved, but in the fact that he was doing it with God's permission - a mistake we make all too often ourselves.

After the blockage, God still allows Balaam to go, but reminds him to ONLY do what God tells him to do. I believe God does the same with us and lets us down the formerly blocked path because we now really get that it's all him and none of us - that he is our only guide - that he is the only thing that should motivate us.

When Balaam was finally in step with God fully (same path, just different control) he goes to Moab and blesses the Israelites and prophesizes the destruction of other nations. Before the third prophesy of Balaam, after feeling the pleasure of the Lord, Numbers 24:2-5 reports that the "Spirit of God came on him" and announced that he was now one who "sees clearly" and "hears the words of God" and "sees a vision of the Almighty" and whose "eyes are open." What a mighty testimony to what can happen if we follow God alone and let him work without our human striving.

Balaam's new direction through God's blockage really spoke to me in my own life, but there was still something there in the story. Numbers 24:25 reports that after giving his prophesies that blessed Israel and foresaw the doom of many of their enemies, that he "left and returned home, and Balak also went on his way." The problem is that the books of Peter, Jude and Revelation refer back to the Balaam story (even though he ended up going the right way) and use it as a negative example, particularly for the church at Pergamum. The reason is that right after Balaam left, while the Israelites were still camped by the people of Moab, "some of the men defiled themselves by having sexual relations with local Moabite women," which then led them to "feast with them and worship the gods of Moab." (Numbers 25:2, NLT) This led to God's wrath on the Israelites which killed 24,000 people. Now we switch to John's word to the church of Pergamum from God in relation to Balaam.

> "But I have a few complaints against you. You tolerate some among you whose teaching is like that of Balaam, who showed Balak how to trip up the people of Israel. He taught them to sin by eating food offered to idols and by committing sexual sin. In a similar way, you have some Nicolatians among you who follow the same teaching. Repent of your sin, or I will come to you suddenly and fight against them with the sword of my mouth."

In Numbers 31:15-17, when Moses gets angry at his people for sparing the women during their revenge on the Midianites (the Midianites were a nomadic group who, at this time in history, were in high numbers among the Moabites). "Why have you let all the women live?" he demanded. "These are the very ones who followed Balaam's advice and caused the people of Israel to rebel against the Lord at Mount Peor. They are the ones who caused the plague to strike the Lord's people." (NLT)

Since it appears plain in the scripture that Balaam left immediately after giving his prophesy, it is not clear how he "advised" or "enticed" Balaak or the Midianite women to "trip up" the Israelites to sin. I'm not sure how the influence came from Balaam, but what is clear is that there is a "teaching" or "spirit of" Balaam that not only enticed the men of Israel to dip their foot in the world, but it is a spirit that affects modern Christianity as well. While Balaam ultimately believed he was following God, he still was influenced by the lures of the world of power, influence and money, and actually convinced himself that he could still follow God's path and power while also having a foothold in what the world deems powerful. This is what happened to the Israelite men, and can so easily happen to us as we become enmeshed in the world to such a degree that we truly believe we are all for God, but convince ourselves that it's ok to dabble in the pursuit of power or wealth. We also gloss over things that are clearly sexual sin because they are so accepted in modern society. This is what I believe was being called out as the spirit or teaching of Balaam that was influencing the church at Pergamum and influences us today.

However, after calling out Balaam in the church, God gives an amazing promise in Revelation 2:17.

> "Anyone with ears to hear must listen to the Spirit and understand what he is saying to the churches. To everyone who is victorious [i.e. has overcome the temptation of the world] I will give some of the manna that has been hidden away in heaven [the special daily provision]. And I will give to each one a white stone, and on the stone will be engraved [made permanent] a new name that no one understands except the one who receives it." (NLT)

What a word from God for those of us who can resist the lure of the world. This is the calling of God for a fulfilling life. It's a new path of relying SOLELY on his daily manna which is preserved for the trusting overcomers. It is our new identity in Him that is so radical that no one in the natural will understand it - but we can't be concerned with that. We just need to take the next step. The step with God that has none of the world mingled in. That is God's destiny for our lives. That is the abundant life. (John 10:10)

♦9♦

"Take What's Rightfully Yours!!!"

The 80's were full of many things, not just bad music (solely my opinion – I was listening to 60's era Bob Dylan at the time), but the rise of greed and materialism in America which (as it will) found its way into the church in the form of the "Name it and Claim it" gospel. While at its heart, this gospel was founded in a pure belief that Jesus could do anything (which He can), its focus on material wealth as a sign of God's favor was misplaced and is in direct contrast to the teaching in the Bible about the dangers of money. Now, in the late 2010's, I see this gospel rising again as we live in a time of prosperity and self focus in which we have created an image of God that reflects our own narcissistic and materially focused belief system. While it is true that "God owns the cattle on a thousand hills" (Psalm 50:10), the context is that "God owns it all and doesn't need anything from us," not "since God is so wealthy, surely he'll bless me with a big chunk of it here on earth." Speaking as someone who made A LOT of money in my prime as an attorney working in a high rise in downtown Los Angeles with a growing 401(K) and a realistic hope of earning 7 figures someday, only to see all my material wealth and security not only disappear, but be replaced with 6 figure debt I had no idea how to pay, I hope I don't really believe (although I'm tempted to) that God's favor was only on me when I had material wealth. While I didn't think I was a "lover of money" when I had it, regularly gave 20% away to my church and good causes, and was generous to my friends and family, when I lost it, I found out very quickly what an idol it had been to me - I was the rich young ruler "walking away sad" because I had "great wealth." (see Matthew 19:22)

We talk a lot in Christian circles about putting God and family first, and not being like the world when it comes to our money, but we all really know that we are - we just avoid the issue because the benefits of wealth are so fun - including our ability to bless others. Clearly God uses Christians with money to do His Kingdom work, and I know numerous wealthy Christians who do not make money their god, but we also need to be real and call it as it is. Today's church is filled with pastors and penitents who are preaching the good news of the gospel of wealth and power instead of the Bible based gospel that says things like "the love of money is the root of all kinds of evil" (1 Timothy 6:10) and that "it is easier for a camel to go through the eye of a needle than for someone who is rich to enter the kingdom of heaven" (Matthew 19:24). We try to avoid these scriptures by saying that money itself is not evil - just the love of it (which is true) or that the "needle" was the name of an ancient type of small gate in Israel (which may be true as well, but only changes Jesus' teaching from impossible to improbable if you've ever been next to a camel which has a head the size of a small sheep).

As one of my dear friend's (Deacon Glenn Harmon of Glenn Harmon Ministries) has been teaching for 25 years at his Catholic Missions across the US and Canada on living an abundant life in Christ, "Our problem is that we don't REALLY believe that God's way is the better way." He's right. We read about money in the Bible (all of which is very clear), we say the right things about not living for money, and we actually judge others who spend money differently than we do as being irresponsible and wasteful. In my experience in marriage mediation, in which I have unfortunately seen a large number of friends (most of which were leaders in the church) either get divorced or have unfulfilling marriages, the biggest seed that takes root to begin cracking what was once a beautiful marriage (apart from the David temptation of sexual lust for what is not rightfully yours) is the lust for money. We work more hours, take less time off, begin a second job, decide that both parents have to work, and lower our ethical standards with regard to taxes or business dealings all for the sake of having more wealth - even when we are already wealthy.

I am clearly not talking about the poor wage earner or single mother who has to work more than they should to just put food on the table, but that is just a small minority of the church. Our pews are filled with the wealthy doing everything in their power to obtain more wealth. God can surely bless us with money, and He does all the time, but when we are living for it (as I have to now confess I was), it can destroy us unless we are blessed like I have been to have it all taken away so I could finally trust "in Christ alone" and really "surrender all" as I had been singing all those years but not really living. Just being real.

Now for my story. I was not much of an athlete in my youth. If you can believe it, my only letter in high school was for being a Mathlete which was our traveling Math team which did word problems against other schools. My letter looked like all the jocks' letters, but had math symbols embroidered into it like π – hence my lack of dating in high school. Having a Mathletes letterman's jacket is not much of a chick magnet wherever you grow up. My three daughters on the other hand, all figured out in Junior High that they were gifted track athletes, my twins Amber and Breean as cross-country runners who were both Southern Section Champions in California, and my youngest daughter Becky as a High Jumper and Heptathlete. All went to wonderful Westmont College in beautiful Santa Barbara, California on scholarship to compete in track on the collegiate level.

While Amber and Breean had very successful high school and college careers in cross country and long distance track and are now wonderful and beautiful 25 year olds living their lives for God, when it came to track, Becky had something special. God gifted her with the ability to jump super high. Since she was 5'10", this meant that high jump was her thing and she loves it more than anything else she does and now can actually jump her own height. The problem is that the high jump is extremely nerve racking as when you jump, all eyes are on you, and you literally have to empty your mind and just trust your training because if you think too much your body can respond poorly and you can tank. This happened to Becky as a senior when she went into the California State Championship as a top-seeded jumper but missed at a very low bar as the pressure of performing on such a big stage was just too much for her young mind. As devastating as that day was for her and our family, it taught her more in one moment than in her entire high school career filled with success. She failed forward.

Becky started her college career with a bang by breaking school records in the heptathlon and high jump in her Freshman year and making the Junior USA Championships. The problem was that for the next three years, while doing extremely well, the time pressures of college life, the highs and lows of relationships, and the instability in our family for the first time in her life due to my money situation and resulting anxiety, she never improved. Her Junior USA high jump mark of 1.78 meters (5' 10") as a Freshman was still her best mark. It is now her Senior year, she is captain of the track team and she wants it bad. So, we headed off to sweaty Gulf Shores, Alabama for the NAIA National Championships to enjoy fried green tomatoes and "throwed" rolls and support our daughter and her team in her final college track meet.

The first two days of the meet could not have gone more smoothly. It was unseasonably cool with low humidity, and Becky killed it ultimately winning the National Championship in the heptathlon - a grueling 2 day competition with 7 events ranging from 100 meter hurdles to shot put to an 800 meter run. She was sore and whooped going into Saturday when the individual open high jump competition would be held against the top athletes in the country. This was the moment in her past when exhaustion and insecurity would creep in, feelings of failure could sneak into her head, and she could miss her mark. All her past failures on the big day came back to her and she had to fight to be in the moment and trust God and the abilities he had given her.

There were 30 qualifiers who made the championship and all began jumping at 1.55 meters (5' 1") - one by one they started to miss as the bar moved up to 1.60 then 1.63, etc. I saw a look of determination and confidence I had not seen in Becky before - plus she was just having fun and enjoying the moment in the midst of the intensity of the moment on a big stage. After making her first six heights, there were now three girls left. One of them was a bit intense and had already announced to all the other competitors that while she had come in 2nd place the year before “this was her year!” They took their first jump - they all missed. They jumped again - they all missed. Now the moment had come. As Becky had missed the least jumps coming to this final height of 1.77 meters - just shy of her best jump ever, she would win by default if all the girls missed on this final height. So, the intense girl jumped - she missed it and fell to the ground in tears. To make matters worse, her coach began yelling at her in front of everyone in one of the worst coaching moments I’ve seen as a parent at a track meet. Becky was now up and it felt like we were living in a movie scene from Chariots of Fire. Everyone is focusing on her, her chief competitor is collapsed on the sidelines crying, the 3rd girl who also hasn’t jumped yet can’t watch so moves behind Becky and turns her back to her. She looks over at me and gives me the sign that she’s ok that we had established in her early days of high jump by swiping her finger over her nose. This is the moment.

Now, to further set the scene, her coach (Josh Priester – who also coaches the Santa Barbara Track Club and its primary athlete Barbara Nwaba who had competed in the Olympic Games in Rio de Jainero, Brazil earlier that year) is standing on the field next to the high jump pit, while the Westmont Head Coach Russell Smelley is sitting with her other teammates and parents outside of the fence just watching and actually eating nachos. He could relax as his other athletes were done, Becky is covered by Coach Priester, and he can finally chill and watch Becky as a spectator. As some background, Coach Smelley is the main reason we sent our girls to Westmont. He is one of the best men I know, coaches with extreme integrity, cares for his athletes like they are his children, and while pushing them to do their best, builds character first above all else. He lost his 14 year old daughter to brain cancer 10 years earlier, then lost his home to a wildfire two years after that, but still preaches God's goodness and redemption. He is also rather introverted and quiet although when one of his athletes needs motivation, he can belt out an encouraging deep yell that can be heard from across the track.

In that moment my stomach is in my throat, Becky's teammates scream their support - then all goes silent as she is ready to make her final jump. Out of the corner of my eye I see movement from the bench where all the other parents are sitting. It's quiet and humble Coach Smelley, having set down his nachos, rising up and moving toward the fence to (what I think) get a closer look. Instead, he puts his hands up to his mouth and yells out in his deep booming voice "BECKY COLLIER – YOU TAKE WHAT'S RIGHTFULLY YOURS!!!" We were all in shock. It was like we were on the Scottish Highlands with Mel Gibson calling us to battle. Well, Becky jumped - made it - the last girl missed, and Becky had her dream. She was the National Champion in her favorite event - the mentally exhausting and technically difficult high jump.

As I sat on the plane ride home reflecting on the meet, Coach Smelley's proclamation brought to mind something I had pushed to the back of my mind after wandering in uncertainty for such a long spell. My wife and I believe that God has given us the gift of being "bridge" people - between old and young, conservative and liberal, and among the races. The biggest bridge area we are called in is regard to the divide that exists between Christian denominations, and our ministry TURN works to bridge that gap through working together for common causes. Over the last 12 years of ministry, we have worked and worshiped with Catholics, Pentecostals, Free Methodists, and Mennonites - all very, very different - but all with one thing in common - loving Jesus in their own unique way.

Part of our connection in the charismatic world brought me to attend a home group in Orange County, Californian, where about 30 people meet every other Wednesday to worship and seek the Lord prophetically - meaning, listen for God's voice about another individual to strengthen and encourage them. Even though I grew up in a denomination that didn't believe that charismatic gifts like tongues or prophesy existed today, I had become a believer five years earlier when I was at the healing rooms at Bethel Church in Redding, California. After finally being called upon for prayer, the leader of the group praying for me randomly asked me, "do you do something with airplanes?" Well, she had me with hello as my profession for my entire career as a lawyer has been exclusively in aviation law.

Now back to the prophetic home group. When I showed up to the group for the first time, I had a sense of anticipation as I had just separated from the partners in my law firm and had no idea what God had for me next. While the agreement to split from my firm was ultimately best for both me and them, there was a lot of resentment and pain (as there will be) and ultimately my partners (through their lawyers) treated me unfairly in many areas having to do with my share of the firm. As I enjoyed this lovely evening of worship there were some encouraging words for me and my wife and son Austin (who became a regular member of this group prior to heading to Ethiopia as a missionary), but nothing crazy or earth shattering. As we broke up and people were getting prayed for a tall African American man I had never met walked up to me and told me that when I had walked in that night God told him something, but he didn't want to say it in public as he sensed it was highly personal and wanted to tell me directly. He then proceeded to tell me that "my partners had taken something that was rightfully mine, but that God wanted to tell me that it was ok and all would be restored to me." I had no idea what this meant, but hearing this from someone who had no idea of my situation, instantly lifted my spirits. I wrote the words in my journal, shared it with close friends, asked God what it meant, but then another two years passed without any form of restoration. The problem was that my tweaked view of God and what he really wants for me tells me that restoration has to do with power or position or money. It is way more than that.

As I look backwards and forwards at age 52, following over two years of uncertainty and battle to find a new identity that is free of the shackles of fame and monetary success, I hear God rising up and yelling the same thing to me - and you as well - wherever you are in life. While we should all be living for our ultimate destiny in heaven, the "cares of the world" keep us in shackles, a veil covers our eyes and we start believing that sex or money or power will give us joy. They don't. Your loving Father - your real life coach - the keeper of the only path to freedom - is screaming out with all the power of heaven – "TAKE WHAT'S RIGHTFULLY YOURS!" Stand up to the world and be different. Live like God's Word is REALLY true! Live the John 10:10 life and then see what your Father can do through you in this world. It's an amazing journey.

♦ 10 ♦

Secret Option "C"

When you battle anxiety (which always comes with resulting depression if not dealt with), you know the feeling. You wouldn't wish it on your worst enemy. What was once a joy is now a burden to be avoided. What was once a place of confidence is now a place of fear and dread. That's where I found myself at age 50 - a man with everything (great family, good friends, loving and beautiful wife, church community, great job), but I was a mess! I was so full of stress and fear that I didn't want to work, started isolating from friends and ultimately became a captive in my own body unable to make the most basic decisions due to fear of failing.

Where anxiety ultimately got me, and where it ultimately gets most people if not dealt with appropriately, is in a hole with absolutely no hope of getting out. In my situation, I had a beautiful home with a pond, basketball and volleyball court. Everyone wanted to come to our house for a party or prayer retreat or dinner/drinks on the back porch. They wanted to bring their kids over to swim or fish. Groups wanted to use our property for retreats and vacation bible school and youth group campouts. It was an oasis in the desert – a place of peace, rest and fun. Most of all though, it was the place I raised my four children. This was where they caught bullfrogs in the pond, played knock-out on the basketball court, played "oh my giddy aunt" in the pool, ate dinner on the back porch at sunset, performed fake weddings with each of my kids and their friends taking a part. This is where we were blessed to live with our best friends and their three kids (and pets) for nine months during their transition into full-time ministry. This is where we held every graduation and birthday party for our kids, as well as our 15th anniversary party. This is where we have held over numerous weddings, the most significant being for my daughter Amber and her sweet husband Jonathan in 2014 where I walked her down the steps into my backyard to hand her over to my two best friends, Dan and Jim, to perform her wedding ceremony with reception to follow on the volleyball court. This was where my other children, and friends' children dream of getting married themselves someday. This is where I planned on playing and fishing and bullfrog hunting with my grandchildren someday.

The problem was that the blessing of my beautiful home and property had also become an idol. It had become part of my identity. I would hear people introduce me as "Alan, the guy with the pond" or "This is Alan - you won't believe his backyard - it's amazing." When something becomes a little too much of your identity, AND you battle insecurity, the thought of losing it is devastating. After losing my job due to stress and struggling with depression resulting from my anxiety and newfound uncertainty, I would find myself sitting on my back porch not enjoying God's creation and blessing to my family, but overcome with worry and fear and regret and shame at being on the verge of losing my blessing. What a loser could I be to become a partner in a law firm and then lose my home. My thought-life got so bad in these dark days that I would see homeless people in my city and really believe that was my lot in life because I had screwed up so badly.

When my first grandchild was born, he was named Tobias which means "God is good." I knew God was good. The problem was that I believed I was bad, not morally, but through my weakness - through not being the man I was called on to be. As much as I loved Toby and was blessed to have lots of time with him during his first six months of life while we babysat him as his mother went to work as a cross-country coach every morning, I was sad. All I could think about was how Toby would not be able to enjoy the blessings of the pond and the zip line. I knew I would be a good grandfather, and had actually already named myself before he was born, but I had failed him - no fishing, no late night bullfrog hunting, no pool basketball, no picking plums and making jam. All the things I had for my children, were now lost to my grandchildren. This was not just a fear, it was a reality. I had lost my job, I was draining my retirement, and I was so racked with anxiety I couldn't fathom starting a new career. The train was heading for a big brick wall of failure and loss. It was inevitable.

I believe in prophetic words from God through people. While they can sometimes be misused, or be so generic they can be for anyone, when they come from a truly prophetic person, it is amazing. I have had a number of words over my life, but only a few stand out, and as I enter into a new season of life in my 50's I am seeing them come to fruition. One word came right after I lost my job, but was still ok emotionally as I was trusting that this was all for good, and that God had a new plan for my life. My wife and I were having dinner with a young couple in Pasadena, California, Andrea and Dustin. Andrea was an old friend we had done ministry with. She was edgy and cool, but had also battled anxiety in her life. She was also super prophetic. As we sat eating dinner, describing ideas of what we could do next in life - work at YWAM, move to England, find a job with an aviation company, become full-time marriage ministers, use our yard for weddings and retreats - Andrea stopped us and said that she felt like God wanted to tell us to stop striving because he had a "Secret Option C for us." I wasn't exactly sure what that meant, but I thought it meant that God had a plan for us that was so unusual we couldn't plan for it in any way other than trusting that He was good and that everything was going to be ok.

Well, let's say you believe God has a secret option C for you. What do you do? I'm not sure. All I know is that my wife Libby did it very well through trust and patience and courage and hope even when things looked really bleak. On the other hand, I tanked. I worried, I complained, I had a pity party, and I began to lose who I really was - a man of faith and freedom and joy. I just wasn't living up to the grandfather name I had given myself.

My wife has wanted to be a grandmother since we were married. I know she adored and cherished all her children, but it was almost like she only wanted kids so she could have grandkids. So, her grandmother name was a big deal to her. Her mother was called Moo Moo for some reason only grandparents can understand. Moo Moo was very beloved and had tons of grandkids and great grandkids before she passed away. When Libby found out our daughter Amber was pregnant, she immediately announced that she would be the new Moo Moo. The only problem was that this was a sacred name in the family and the kids flat out rejected it. It would be like a Dodger wanting to wear the number 42 - it just was not going to happen. So, she began trying different versions of Moo Moo like Mee Mee and Ma Ma and Moo Lan and Moo Shu – but nothing worked. Finally, she had a revelation from the Lord and announced to the world (without consultation) that on the day Toby was born, she would officially be known as Ma Moo (pronounced like Shamu from Sea World).

The children laughed and poked fun at her (as they will), but whatever I thought about the name, I knew she had made the decision and that was that. I consider myself a fairly funny guy. My dry sense of humor gets me in trouble sometimes, but also brings me life. One of my favorite things to do is to be sarcastic where I say something ridiculous with a straight face and good back up and see if gullible people (like my sweet wife) believe me. For my children's sake (who think I'm funny too), all I'll say is that their mom does not appreciate the fact that I am fluent in sarcasm.

With my tragic flaw in mind, and my sweet wife now wanting to be called Ma Moo for the rest of her life, it was time to pick my grandparent name. While I was open to whatever Libby wanted to be called (even though I might poke fun at her at times), I was firm on one thing - she was not naming me one of her ridiculous names like Pa Pa or Poo Poo. I was also not going to be boring old Granddad. I wanted to be something special and silly. I also wanted to mess with my wife a little. I therefore announced at a family gathering that I had prayed long and hard and that I really felt led to not just be called a normal name by my soon to be first grandson, and the hopefully many grandchildren to follow, but wanted to be called something unique and dynamic and meaningful. I wanted to not just be a name but a sound - PING!!!!!! You know, like a submarine. That was it! I was now Grandpa Ping. Well, although it was sort of a joke at the time to mess with my wife through sarcasm, when the big day came and my beautiful grandson Toby was born, Libby held him close and whispered into his ears. "Ma Moo loves you." I had to follow suit, so I whispered "Grandpa Ping loves you too." What was at first just a moment of silliness was now my official grandparent name like it or not. Well I not only like it - I love it. I even decided to use it in my yearly jam making ritual with my newly named "Grandpa Ping's Organic Fantastic Homemade Jam." And, as a testament to my dear wife, when Toby finally began to speak, he couldn't say Ma Moo - it just came out "Moo Moo" - just like she wanted (and probably secretly planned) all along. I am now Ming – close enough.

Now back to Secret Option "C." In the midst of my anxiety and resulting depression, I knew I ultimately needed to get back to work - I just didn't know what to do. I definitely didn't want to go back to the law firm life with its endless hours and stress. I loved aviation law, but what job could I possibly get at my age if I really didn't want to litigate any longer, and I wanted to be free in my 50's, doing something I was passionate about. The problem was that I loved our ministry TURN, but there was really no way to make enough money there - that needed to be an add-on to my main job as I supported my wife in her calling to help the needy. Everyone in my world - except prophetic Andrea - was telling me and Libby that I

HAD TO move forward doing SOMETHING. They were right from a worldly responsible perspective as we were running out of money, had just put our house on the market but had no idea where we were going to live let alone how we were going to pay for it. So, I looked into working for a large non-profit, I applied at Trader Joes where I heard they hired people my age and it was fun and relaxing (but only paid a low hourly rate), and I even took one of my dear friends up on his offer to try out selling windows. These were all noble and healthy moves forward for me in my stuck state, but even though the clock was ticking, I just knew none of these were right. It was striving, when God (now that I had stepped out in faith) wanted me to wait for my Secret Option "C."

Then it happened - after two years of uncertainty and KNOWING in my mind that I would never be able to duplicate the good parts of my old job as an aviation law firm partner (even though it had been slowly taking my life), the sky opened up for me. It's way too long of a story to tell, but one thing after another started waking me up and giving me confidence again. It started with a call from a friend who had heard Disney was looking for an aviation lawyer to deal with the risk involved with their use of drones as well as amusement park flyovers. After sending them my resume and talking to the hiring executive for parks I started to realize how much I loved aviation and analyzing how to manage and prevent risk as a company. Even though the job ended up being in Orlando, so that was a non-starter, it had lit a flame inside me. Then, I got a call from a friend of mine named Tom who was involved with construction risk who told me that he wanted to move away from his job full of travel and stress to something new, but that he didn't want to do it on his own, and saw me as a perfect person to partner with as we had a passion for helping companies prevent risk but also had the same exact sense of humor that drove our wives crazy. I really didn't know what such a partnership could look like, but I was all in.

Now remember, I still don't have a job, and although my wife had creatively figured out a way for our non-profit to be compensated for the great work it did in our city, we were far from being able to pay our mortgage. Even if our house sold for a good price, all the equity would be going to college debt. Well, about three weeks after that call from Tom, we found ourselves traveling together to Gulf Shores Alabama to watch our children compete in the NAIA National Track Championships - my daughter Becky in high jump and heptathlon (see last chapter) and his son Daniel (aka "HD") in the javelin. As we had to fly into New Orleans and drive three hours to and from Gulf Shores, Tom and I had loads of time to talk and were beginning to share both of our somewhat dire financial situations, including the fact that I was selling my house (even though I didn't want to), but had no place to live. When we finally got back to New Orleans, we had a few hours before our flight back to California, so we visited the historic district. Our wives went off to explore shops, and we walked over to the Mississippi to walk along the shore and chat. It was then that Tom finally opened up about his desire to have his youngest son be able to run track at Westmont College like his two older brothers which had been his dream. However, if his son was going to go to this expensive private college, he was going to have to face some pretty serious new debt and wasn't sure if he was going to be able to afford his mortgage.

Tom and his wife Angela live in a beautiful location in Northern San Diego County called Poway. While all of Poway is beautiful, they live in the most special part of town up in the mountains in a forest of scrub oaks, with a stream running through it, overlooking beautiful Lake Poway which is just a twelve minute walk through the woods down to the lakefront. For those unfamiliar with Southern California, Poway is twenty minutes from Del Mar and thirty minutes from downtown San Diego. It became infamous in 2003 when the Cedar Fire swept through town and wiped out a number of homes. Tom and Angela's home survived the fire but the large barn on their two acre property was destroyed. They made the best of it, took the insurance money and rebuilt a new barn, but this one was special - it had an upstairs game room with a pool table and entertainment area, and a downstairs where friends could stay with a lovely bedroom and living room and outdoor deck on both floors overlooking the forest. As Tom is a builder, the barn was not only lovely, it was built like a tank with six inch block walls and fireproof everything - no fire was going to take this barn out. He even marked the barn with an emblem for his last name McCollum putting a very subtle "M" on the front of the barn with a big "C" in the middle. When Tom built the barn, he wanted to ultimately build a place for someone to live with a beautiful indoor/outdoor kitchen and extra bedroom, but he didn't have the money to finish it. Also, in order to get the permit to rebuild the barn, the City of Poway required him to sign a covenant to never rent out the barn as a landlord.

So, Tom was in a quandary. He and Angela had decided to not allow fear to stop them from allowing their son to go to Westmont College, but they weren't exactly sure how the money thing was going to work out. As Tom looked at his finances, he decided that in the worst case scenario, he could rent out his house (no covenant) and move into the beautiful barn house. Not perfect, but it would preserve his property until things hopefully improved financially. As he told me this story during our sweaty walk down the river, Tom got a gleam in his eyes that I believe was straight from the Holy Spirit and announced, "Alan, would you want to live in our barn?" Well, I loved that barn and knew that once the extra work was done, it would not only be an ok place to live, but a dream. Plus, it was a win-win, as we could bless Tom and Angela with some money to build out the barn and live there every month. The amount they needed us to pay to help them cover their new college costs were below what it would cost us to rent an apartment in our old town. On top of that, we got to live next door to our new very dear friends. We both knew this was God, told our wives who felt it too, and headed back to San Diego Airport and then Poway where we would be sleeping in the barn before heading back to our home town of Riverside the next morning. Now for the crescendo - when I woke the next morning, I headed to the upper deck of the barn for some early morning quiet time. As I sat down with my Bible, I was not only struck with the beauty of this barn in the woods, but with the rushing stream below and the abundance of doves flying around almost as a kiss from God saying the Holy Spirit was in this place in a big way. After spending some time with God, I headed down the road to the McCollum's house to grab a cup of coffee. On my walk back I looked up at the front of the barn which I had never studied closely because it was night the other times I was there. And then it hit me - because the McCollum "M" was so subtle, all that stood out on the front of the barn was a big letter "C." Not only was that the first letter of our last name - but God was hitting me right between the eyes with my destiny – this was my Secret Option "C"

The rest of the story is still playing out, but involves a new life as a consultant in aviation, a new vibrancy in our non-profit, new connections in our beloved second country of Uganda, and an amazing discovery that our house was in demand as a vacation rental which would cover our mortgage. I'm not sure how long God will keep us there, but for now, it is such a blessing as we enjoy our new community, hike around the lake every day, and re-live our early marriage years. Yes, the impossible became possible - my regret and shame had become my hope and glory - my grandchildren didn't only still get to enjoy the home their parents were raised in, they also had the new Moo Moo and Grandpa Ping's new home - the barn on the lake - Secret Option "C."

♦ 11 ♦

Captain Awesome

After being married for 5 years, finally graduating law school and being a year into my new job as a trial lawyer in downtown Los Angeles, my wife and I knew it was time to start fulfilling our dream of having a big family. We both loved kids and wanted lots of them - our plan was six - it worked for the Brady Bunch, so why not us. Three boys and three girls - perfect.

When Libby got pregnant after a romantic trip to Puerto Vallarta, she quickly started growing. When I say growing, I mean that within three months she looked full term, at six months she was attracting unwanted attention. At one point, we waddled into a movie theater and a well-doer turned around in her seat and told us to "rest easy" as she was a nurse - just in case the excitement of the movie triggered her into labor. "How far along are you?" she asked. "Four months." "Wow – you're huge!" "Thanks." Libby was from a family of twins. Her mom was a twin, her brother had twins, and it was her lifelong dream to crank out two puppies at one time. We even talked about it while we were dating. So, when she told me she thought she was having twins, despite the doctor's insistence that he only heard one heartbeat, I just chalked it up to wishful thinking. But she was persistent. Every time someone asked her what she thought she was having, she would answer "twins." Since we believed in being as natural as possible, and because ultrasound was not considered as safe as it is now some 25 years later, we waited to get a scan until Libby was entering her fifth month. I wouldn't normally have taken off work and gone with her for an ultrasound, but I was nervous she would just start crying when it was confirmed there was only one baby in her. Well, we went to the doctor's office, she laid out on the table, had goop spread all over her belly, and the nurse started scanning. One minute, two minutes … now Libby was getting anxious. Was there something wrong? Why is the nurse so silent?

Then she said, "Do you know that there are two babies in here?" After much screaming, jubilation, and "I told you so's" to the doctor, the adventure began with our two girls, dubbed Baby "A" and Baby "B" - now the amazing and beautiful Amber and Breean.

Three years later, Libby thought she was having twins again, but this time it was only a humongous 10 lbs 5 oz third daughter delivered naturally even though she was what is called a "compound presentation," which means her hand was over her head as my wife supernaturally delivered not only her large Collier head, but her shoulder as well. Again, because my wife is what a British client's girlfriend once called an "earth mother," we didn't want the sac broken artificially, so (being that it was Becky in there), it just grew and grew during delivery coming out like a freaky white balloon of tissue. When the doctor finally cut it open out of necessity, my sweet daughter's hand was reaching out into her new world with the doctor announcing "shake your daughter's hand," a prophetic first jump over the high bar.

As Becky was born looking two years old, we loved our new set of triplets, and were having the time of our lives, but deep down, I really wanted a son - or three to keep pace with our master Brady plan. So, when it was time to try for another child (less than a year later), we actually read books on "how to conceive a boy." Sorry, no detail here. See Chapter Five. When Libby found out she was pregnant, we had sadly lost our sweet natural doctor to cancer, and needed a new plan. At this point, Libby was a childbirth consultant and teacher for the Bradley method, and was determined to have a home birth despite this being a second VBAC (look it up) and her having VLB's (figure it out). To make matters more exciting, Libby announced one date night evening that she had not only invited her parents to be at the birth together with our three daughters and two best friends, but that the founders of Bradley had asked whether they could film the birth for a new training video. Whatever, bring it on!

The birth was going beautifully with no complications, but we still didn't know the sex of our soon to be fourth child as we wanted it to be a surprise. When the time came, the midwife told me to get in position to catch the baby. After grabbing hold of this gloopy bundle of joy, I heard Libby's sweet father yell out "It's a boy!" "It's a boy!" "It's a little boy!" We don't have Walter anymore, but because of the never to be released footage of the birth, we have that moment forever on film. I cry every time I see it. Well, we now had our family - not six like Mr. Brady, but a solid four with Amber and Breean, Becky and Austin Herschel (the Majestic Deer) weighing in at a whopping 10 lbs 11 oz. Austin has been sweet, gentle and funny since he was born. I don't know if it's because he had to deal with three sisters who shaved his legs, locked him in the shed naked and dressed him like a girl for music videos, but he was just a calm and collected little guy - our family mascot.

In 2006, when Austin was only nine, Libby and I traveled to Uganda to do a project with World Vision at the tail end of the atrocities committed by Joseph Kony in Northern Uganda (more in another chapter). During this life-changing trip, we were blessed one night to be at a prayer gathering with Dennis Odoi of World Vision, two other local prayer warriors and Dennis' cousin Florence who had gone to Gulu with us (and also was nicknamed Lazurus as she had been raised from the dead - again, see Africa chapter). I've shared some of the amazing prophetic words over my journey the last three years, but at that point in my life, I had not experienced any first-hand. During the hour long prayer time, a lot of words were spoken over my wife and I and what God was doing in Uganda, but one stood out, and I wrote it down in my journal - it was from Lazarus. "One of your twins - and your youngest - will be used mightily by God!" Then, after being told it was a son, she proclaimed - "He will preach to many people and lead thousands to Jesus!"

At this point in his life, Austin was not necessarily exhibiting the traits of someone who was going to be a great preacher or missionary. He was tall and slightly awkward, with inherited bad Collier teeth, and had trouble reading, which was later diagnosed as dyslexia. With his older sisters super-achieving in academics and sports, I noticed that the poor little guy started becoming self conscious and insecure in himself no matter what we told him - a trait he unfortunately inherited from his daddy. Well, one Saturday when we were visiting our dear friends the Glasners in Thousand Oaks, I felt as if God told me to wake up early and take Austin on an early morning hike up to a rocky hilltop in Simi Valley at Corriganville Ranch. A few years earlier, I had had an encounter with God at this same spot. At that time, I just found out I was to be the next partner at my law firm, and I was totally freaking out. I climbed up that mountain, laid down on the rock and just stared at the clouds blowing in the wind. In that moment, I felt God telling me that he was in control and to just relax and let him flow like the clouds. My dad then called randomly and told me that God had told him to call me and tell me to be "Strong and Courageous!" right out of Joshua 1:9.

So, we got up at 6:00 am, drove over to Corriganville, and started our ascent. On the way up, I told Austin to watch out "in the Spirit" as Satan did not want what was about to take place to happen. As soon as those words left my mouth, Austin spotted a dust devil spinning through our path and woke up to the fact that this was a serious spiritual moment. When we got to the top, other than being beautiful, nothing happened right away. I told Austin what my dad had told me - that God was calling him to be "Strong and Courageous!" and that he was called to great things not because of who he was but for the fact that God wanted to use him. Then it happened. A swarm of at least 100 hornets appeared instantly in front of us just over the cliff of the rock just hovering and watching us. When God is moving, you really just have to listen and be obedient so I asked Austin if he believed he had God's power in him. He said yes. I then told him to stretch out his arm and command those hornets to go in the name of Jesus! Well, he reached out his little hand, commanded those hornets to go, and lo and behold a blast of wind swept behind us and blew those hornets away. I don't get it - but it happened. We then high-tailed it out of there, but as we looked back, there was a shaft of light shining through the clouds at just the point we had been - a reminder that God is in control and had a plan for Austin's life.

God's hand in Austin's life was reconfirmed about a year later when we traveled to Long Island, New York to be with my family for Christmas. Earlier that year, I had met a woman from the Native Cree Nation of Canada at a reconciliation conference. Rita was the sister of one of my wife's spiritual mentors named Fern Noble, a mighty prayer warrior especially in the area of reconciliation and forgiveness. Our family uses the term "Cree" based upon Fern's tender, gracious and giving nature. Not only do you need to be careful complimenting any of Fern's clothes or possessions (as if you do, you will likely find it wrapped as a gift for you the next morning), but she is so sensitive to people's feelings that even if you say something to her that is wrong factually, she just smiles and makes you think you're Wikipedia. One time she was at a conference with her friend (author and our dear friend Fawn Parrish) when someone she didn't know walked up to her and said "Hi Fawn, I really love your book *Honor*! Would you sign my copy?" Instead of embarrassing her by telling her she not only wasn't Fawn, but looked absolutely nothing like her Caucasian friend, she just said "Thank you so much! That really means a lot to me!" She then signed the book on Fawn's behalf and told her the story a few hours later.

In our family, particularly in our marriage, if someone is telling a story and gets a fairly meaningless fact wrong, like a date, or name, or other irrelevant detail, it is so tempting to correct them and not only interrupt their flow, but actually potentially embarrass them in front of friends or family. So, if someone gives into the weakness and corrects someone in the middle of the story, we are very quick to correct them and say "That wasn't Cree!" Try it - it's a very helpful tool in marriage. You can wait to correct the mistake later in a different setting, or just, like Fern, let it go.

When I met Rita for the first time, I found out that she not only was an awesome worship leader using her handmaid deerskin drum, but she was a gifted craftswoman, as she actually made drums as a way of earning extra income. During worship one night at the conference, I felt a nudge from God that I was supposed to get one of Rita's drums for Austin and find a way to draw on it a picture of our experience on the mountain in Simi Valley. Rita, being Cree, just gave me a drum, and I proceeded to draw a picture of a mountain with Austin standing on top with wind coming from him and driving away the wasps stating "Be Strong and Courageous!" I then decided that it was important at this stage of life for Austin to get a blessing from his grandfather and father - passing our mantel of faith from my dad through me to my only son. When we arrived in New York it was cold and snowy, but we found a time for my dad Wally, Austin and I to take the long hike into the woods near his house in Rocky Point, NY to his prayer rock - a very special place where my mom's ashes were later buried. We didn't tell Austin what was going on until we got there, but when we arrived, I not only gave him his new drum, but my dad and I prayed a blessing over him, passing our mantel of faith onto him for the next generation of Collier men in my line of the family. As we ended our prayer I heard a noise, looked up and saw a flock of geese flying overhead in a perfect "V" - a further confirmation of God's blessing over the victory in Austin's life. He then climbed up on the rock and played his drum and if you can believe it, was instantly lit up by the sun as the clouds broke open - a kiss from God to his son.

Austin proceeded through adolescence after that, being a great kid, but battling his learning disability and resulting insecurity. He somehow tested into the excellent and high academic Christian school our girls had achieved so well at, but now, at age 17, he was faltering. The school and teachers loved Austin - they just couldn't figure out how to deal with him. When he couldn't do an "easy" word scramble in class, his teacher gave him zeros. When he couldn't quite get reading comprehension - almost impossible for someone with dyslexia - they wouldn't give him oral exams. He just failed. I don't blame the school as they were just ignorant, but at that point in his life, the only thing he was confident in was his athletics. He was super tall and was becoming dominant in volleyball and basketball while also following his sisters' footprints in track and field. But he couldn't maintain a C average, so guess what - school rules - no sports. Now he was not only insecure about academics, he was embarrassed as all his friends were asking why he wasn't on the team anymore. In his insecurity, he sometimes mumbled, so on at least three occasions - one being my mom's wake - people asking him his name really thought he had told them he was "Awesome" - also prophetic.

At this point we had had it as parents, pulled him out of school and started him on a fantastic home school program in which he learned in a different way - by sharing in a circle of his classmates. He began to get his mojo back. That September of 2014, Libby and I were headed off to our yearly trip to an aviation conference and on to Munich and London for my business, and Austin was going to be home alone for 10 days during his spring break. Austin's cousin Mariah and her husband Sage were in Kona, Hawaii with YWAM (Youth With a Mission) which trains and then sends young people to serve God overseas. They invited Austin to visit. It's his story to tell, but at that point in his life he was battling a lot of demons including depression and anxiety. After experiencing the amazing YWAM culture in Kona for a few days, he was excited but still waiting for something, almost afraid for God to draw near as He might see his flaws as a young man. Following an outdoor night of worship, Austin started praying and actually looked down at his shadow ashamed at what he "believed" he had become. Then Sage walked up and asked him if he needed prayer. During that prayer, Austin fell to the ground with what people call being slain in the Spirit. He didn't get up for over an hour during which time Jesus talked to him directly, told him he was proud of him and showed him visions for what he was to become.

The rest is history in the making, as Austin came home, announced he wanted to graduate a year early and go to discipleship training school (DTS) in Kona with YWAM. He left a year later, went to Turkey to minister for three months, received further leadership training to go into the mission field long term, and is now based in Ethiopia where this little insecure kid who couldn't make a C average, has learned the local language Amharic and is a leader in his team in Addis Abbaba where he regularly sees the miraculous power of God. His boldness and faith are staggering! He is "Strong and Courageous!" and that Lazarus prophesy when he was nine is in full force as he approaches his 21st birthday.

Now to the punch-line. I have always been a slightly silly, sometimes inappropriate, but always creative and fun dad to my kids, but I got my training by babysitting. My best gig ever was when Libby and I were dating and we had the pleasure of babysitting our friend's (the Deegans) four kids every Friday night while they had date night. I was in charge of putting Robert and John Michael down (age seven and nine), while Libby did Jenny and little Gracie. The boys demanded stories at bedtime so I obliged - mainly involving super heroes I had made up. One night I decided to bring over a puppet made in youth group many years earlier that had a furry body and big thick felt eyes. As I was doing the dinner dishes and they were taking baths, I found two old fashioned rubber bottle nipples in the dirty dishes (for baby Gracie) and realized that they fit perfectly over the felt eyes of my puppet. A small dish towel cape later, and "Nipple Eyes" was born. My stories of "Nipple Eyes and the Naked Surfing Grandpas" and "Big Scary Lady" became big hits and I took them (to my wife's chagrin) into my night-time ritual with my kids.

Flash-forward to August of 2017 which is when I'm writing this chapter. Following my retirement from my law firm, and prior to becoming full-time as a consultant, we had time to travel, so we decided to take the first three weeks in August to go to Ethiopia to visit Austin then take him to visit our dear friends in Uganda, including Florence (who had prophesied about him those many years before) as well as Ammabel and Brian Rushaju who do wonderful work for less fortunate in their country. When we arrived at the Rushaju's house in Bamba, we were greeted by their four exuberant boys aged three through nine. During the week, the boys reminded me that my daughter Becky (who has visited Uganda twice doing micro-finance loan projects with needy women and stayed with the Rushaju's), had told them about "Bottle Eyes" (edited for conservative Uganda) and that she promised that I would share a story one night when I was there.

As we had traveled South with the Rushajus during our visit to the beautiful home town of Brian called Kabale, we were able to run through a national park where we saw zebras, giraffes, and hippos. As my only experience had been the twirling ears of the harmless robotic creatures at Disneyland's Jungle Cruise, Austin's announcement that hippos were the most dangerous animals in Africa was surprising news. We quickly realized that he actually had a minor phobia about hippos for which he was made fun of by me and the Rushaju boys for all the five hour drive back to Bomba. It was now our last night with the boys.

They were all over me to tell them the much anticipated and promised story, so I brought Austin into the boys bunk-filled room and began a story about the origin of Bottle Eyes - just an insecure little squeaky voiced kid named Mike Milky. But when he yelled "Mooky Moo!!!" he transformed into a mighty milk squirting superhero! On this occasion, Bottle Eyes was faced with a force too powerful even for him – "Demon Hippos from the Deep" who used their Djbouti's (private Africa joke) to pummel Bottle Eyes to the point of near death. Until, out of the sky came a savior. A superhero friend who had overcome his fear of hippos to fly in (and with his magic hammock) save the day - and Bottle Eyes. His name was Captain Awesome!

♦ 12 ♦

Handsome Deer Coal Carrier

I'm very proud of my name! Even though I was the second born son in my family, my dad wanted his first son (my brother Stephen Wallace) to have his name, and because I was born with black hair like my mom's father, I was chosen on that Christmas Day in 1964 to receive his name - Herschel. I have no idea how a Protestant English/Scottish family like my mom's got a Hebrew name in their lineage, but there it was, ready to be passed down to me (and then my son). I never met my maternal grandfather as he died of a brain tumor when my mom was only ten, but I know that he was a printer, that he was very athletic and loved sports (especially tennis), that he had a 1916 Howard 19 jewel pocket watch that was his prized possession passed down to him from his uncle (and now to me), and that my grandmother (who we called Nana) was madly in love with him. She remarried twice after Herschel - Homer (heart attack) and Clint - our beloved Pop who loved my grandmother dearly for over 20 years. Although Pop was impotent from a vasectomy mishap at the time they married, my Nana didn't seem to mind - as long as he sat in as her Rook partner once in a while and drove them to church - she was good. Neither later husband (Pop for good reason) would ever quite match up to the passion that was Nila and Herschel. My grandmother would often share with me (in front of Pop) Hershel's prowess as a man and how romantic their marriage was. Pop would just smile in his soft way, get his Pringles and Coke and go back to fixing watches in the back room.

As I became an adult and the age of the internet began, a search one morning led me to the realization that my middle name meant "deer" in Hebrew. As Psalm 62 ("As a deer pants for streams of water ...") is one of my favorites, I was happy to have deer in the middle of my name. I then found out my first name Alan meant "handsome" - also very acceptable to me who had lived through childhood and adolescence being very sensitive to my large (size 8) head and prominent ears. The one part of my name I did know about was Collier as I had been told from childhood that it was an English name that meant coal miner. In fact, the Colliers were from Northern Central England and were "coal carriers" meaning they toted the coal (made from wood) from town to town. Our most famous shout out in history is from William Shakespeare who follows the famous Prologue of Romeo and Juliet ("Two households …") as follows: "Gregory, o' my word, we'll not carry coals." Gregory's brilliant response: "No, for then we should be colliers." I don't really get it, but hey, it's pretty cool. So now my name - Handsome Deer Coal Carrier. My son Austin - Majestic Deer Coal Carrier. His son - something Deer Coal Carrier.

I love the story of Gideon in the Bible. It is a story of overcoming insecurity and accepting how God sees you. The story comes from the book of Judges, chapters 6-8 and tells of a time when all of Israel was in hiding because they were being attacked by the "cruel" Midianites. When the Israelites finally called out to God for help, He responded by sending an angel who "came and sat down under the oak in Ophrah that belonged to Joash the Abiezrite, where his son Gideon was threshing wheat in a winepress to keep it from the Midianites" - meaning he was hiding in fear. Then, the angel appeared to Gideon in the place of his hiding and said, "The Lord is with you mighty warrior." After then asking how the Lord was "with them" in the midst of their suffering, "[t]he Lord turned to him and said, "Go in the strength you have and save Israel out of Midian's hand. Am I not sending you?" Gideon then questioned the new name he had been given by God through his insecurity about his family name and position - "Pardon me, my Lord, … but how can I save Israel? My clan is the weakest in Manasseh, and I am the least in my family." Then, of course, as we will, Gideon asked God for a sign it was really Him, and the angel burned up his sacrifice so impressively that Gideon finally realized he was dealing with an angel and said, "Alas, Sovereign Lord! I have seen the angel of the Lord face to face!"

However, even after this, when the battle actually came and he was fulfilling his call to leadership, Gideon asked God for another sign to confirm if He would actually "save Israel by my hand as you have promised…." A couple of wet and dry fleeces later, he finally had to accept his new name and take a step of faith, and of course,

God was true to His word and the Midianites were defeated by the coward turned mighty warrior. Isn't this just like us. God is calling us to new things, to new names beyond our heritage, our education, our wealth, our strength, but we waver, we doubt, we ask for more and more signs. But when we finally wake up - God can do things through us that we could have never imagined.

This promise of a new name beyond anything we could ever see in ourselves is explained further in Revelation 2:17 (which is touched on at the end of Chapter 8) in the perplexing story of Balaam and his donkey. It is revealed to Paul that for those who are victorious over the power of the world, God will not only give his "special" provision - the "hidden manna" but also "a white stone with a new name written on it, known only to the one who receives it." When I first heard a teaching on this scripture, the pastor explained that while this was likely a promise set aside for us in heaven, he called upon our congregation to ask God to reveal his special name to us - the name that reveals what we are meant to be - like that given to Peter and to Gideon. One morning I did just that - I asked, I waited, and I got it - He called me "Gentle Warrior." This was significant in my role as a lawyer as I did need to fight, but I needed not to lose the spirit of my earthly father who always had a gentle spirit (often to his detriment as people often took advantage of his trusting and giving nature). Years later this name was confirmed as a prophetic woman was praying over me and said God was calling me "Gentle Warrior."

The problem was that sometimes as a trial attorney, you can fall into the trap of many lawyers who succeed in their profession by being complete asses (like Balaam's friend). I tried it often and it worked. This moved into my non-lawyer world as well when my worldly arrogance would slip into judgment of others, cutting humor, and caddy responses to what I viewed as ignorant questions or comments. It got so bad during my "confident" lawyer years that some of my dear friends (who still loved me) started calling me "assquire" a good description of how I was acting at times. Where I should have responded in repentance to this teasing, I actually liked it - it somehow gave me strength and protection from the reality of my insecurity. When I crashed emotionally in 2015 this arrogance left as well. Now that God has taken me through the death and burial described in other chapters of this book, and I enter into my resurrection period (the final stage of what my Catholic friends call the Paschal Mystery) and gain a new confidence as doors begin to fly open again, I have to remember that I still stink a bit and need to remember where God pulled me out of.

So, while I am so proud of being a "Herschel" and passing it down to my son, grandson and beyond, I need to always fight the temptation to embrace my assquire nature and grab onto what it means to be Adiv Gavriel - the Gentle Warrior!

♦ 13 ♦

The Outer Wall

I was blessed a few years ago to travel to Israel with my youngest daughter and son to visit our older daughter who was studying abroad in the Middle East. There were many highlights of the trip, but one of my most enjoyable times was going through what is known as Hezekiah's Tunnel near the old City of David with my son Austin. This curving underground tunnel is 533 meters (1748 feet running from the Gihon Spring to the Pool of Siloam), filled with moving ankle deep water, has no lighting other than the souvenir pen lights, and is a challenge for anyone with even a hint of claustrophobia or for a father and son both over 6' 2", but it is also a fun adventure and a real taste of history. The tunnel was built at the time of King Hezekiah during the threat to Jerusalem by the invading King Sennacherib of Assyria. The city of Jerusalem at the time was built on a mountain and naturally defensible, but its weakness was that its major source of fresh water (the Gihon Spring) was located on the side of a cliff overlooking the Kidron Valley, leaving it outside of the walls and vulnerable to invading armies.

2 Chronicles 32:2-4 records the Assyrian threat and the vulnerability of the Spring as follows:

> "When Hezekiah saw that Sennacherib had come and that he intended to wage war against Jerusalem, he consulted with his officials and military staff about blocking off the water from the springs outside the city, and they helped him. They gathered a large group of people who blocked all the springs and the stream that flowed through the land. 'Why should the kings of Assyria come and find plenty of water?' they said."

The Bible then records in verse 30 that "It was Hezekiah who blocked the upper outlet of the Gihon spring and channeled the water down to the west side of the City of David." 2 Kings 20:20 later records, "As for the other events of Hezekiah's reign, all his achievements and how he made the pool and the tunnel by which he brought water into the city, are they not written in the book of the annals of the kings of Judah?" Then Isaiah, as part of his prophesy (found in Isaiah 22:11) about the fate of Jerusalem reflects, "You built a reservoir between the two walls for the water of the Old Pool, but you did not look to the One who made it or have regard for the One who planned it long ago." Although Hezekiah thought of it, and engineers made it happen, God ordained it "long ago."

As I was reading the 2 Chronicles report of Sennacherib's threat recently, I noticed something for the first time. After directing his people to block the water and apparently build the tunnel to connect the Gihon Spring to what became the Pool of Siloam inside the city walls, he did three other things:

> "Then he worked hard repairing all the broken sections of the wall and building towers on it. He built another wall outside that one and reinforced the terraces of the City of David." (2 Chronicles 32:5 NIV)

In preparation for the attack of the enemy, Hezekiah (1) repaired the city walls that had broken, (2) built towers on those walls, and (3) built an outer wall. As I reflected on this, I was struck by the fact that Hezekiah's preparation for an inevitable attack of the enemy provides a symbolic insight into one of the greatest attacks on men of faith today - sexual sin - and how to protect against it so that they will not be overcome by the enemy.

The Attack of the Enemy through Sexual Sin

In my experience as a lay marriage counselor and men's group leader, I have seen no greater threat to Christian men, and particularly male Christian pastors and leaders, than sexual temptation. From Jimmy Swaggart to Ted Haggard in the evangelical movement to the much publicized issues surrounding priests in the Catholic Church, we are bombarded with the impact of moral failure in Christian leaders in the area of sexuality.

Interestingly, the attack on Jerusalem in the time of Hezekiah was by the king Sennacherib whose name literally means "Sîn sends many brothers." The Sîn referred to here is not the word we use to refer to disobeying God's laws, but rather to the god of the moon in Mesopotamian mythology symbolized by the horns of a bull. Sîn later became a Semitic god which many believe was the focus of worship when the Israelites created the golden calve as Moses was atop Mount Sinai getting the ten commandments.

The city of Jerusalem was under attack by the seemingly unstoppable force of a king named for the god who tempted God's people at a time when their leader was not only meeting God face to face, but getting the laws that would shape their relationship with Him. Men of faith today are under attack by an even more formidable enemy - one that can not only destroy their family, but steal their soul. However, like the people at the base of Mount Sinai, we somehow get totally blinded to the wages of our sin, and so easily fall prey to the temptations of the flesh.

Repairing the Broken Wall

We all have walls of protection in our walk of faith to protect us from falling into the temptation of sexual sin. Just like Hezekiah - if we are reflective, we quickly notice that these walls are broken in many ways, and often have some gaping holes that the enemy can walk right through. One of these holes I have noticed in Christian men over the years is when they choose to do something (running, having regular coffee/lunch dates, going to the theater, etc.) with someone other than your spouse. When confronted with this issue, men (and their wives) often chalk it up to the fact that the husband has an interest that his wife doesn't (but a woman friend does), and that since the wife knows about it, it's totally ok. In many instances, the "other" woman is a friend of the wife making it even more innocent. Well, while it may start innocently, I have seen a number of marriages fail (or almost fail) because one thing leads to another and the emotional bond of these "friends" with common interests leads to an emotional and/or sexual affair that is hard to overcome. While the Billy Graham rule of never being alone with a woman is extreme, I recommend a version of that rule which says that I will never choose to do something alone with a person of the opposite sex that I should be doing with my wife. If my wife can't or doesn't enjoy doing that activity, I should find another man to do it with or just do it solo.

The second serious wall problem is in the area of porn which has become an epidemic in the Christian community and is a serious threat to our relationship with God and our spouse. There is just one answer to this problem - cut it off entirely or if you can't, seek help before it gets such a hold on you it's too late. If you follow this rule and begin seriously investing in emotional and sexual intimacy with your wife and your wife alone, your wall of protection can withstand the battering rams that come after your marriage that want to take you out.

Watchtowers

The second way Hezekiah prepared for the enemy attack was by building watchtowers around the city walls. Even though he knew the attack was coming, it was vital to be on watch at all times or the enemy could sneak up on him. This is true in the defense against sexual sin. As a man can so easily slip into temptation from a sneak attack (that comes out of nowhere in many cases) it is imperative to have close friends who are part of your life and who will keep you accountable. These watchmen will notice when you speak about another woman too much, when you share that you have decided to lose weight by jogging and have chosen to run with a female friend since you wife is not "into it," when you travel away from home all the time on business trips and never include your spouse, when they sense that you and your wife are not emotionally connected, or when your wife tells their wife that you are not interested in sex anymore. These are all signs of an attack, but men are often ignorant to it until the enemy gets through the wall and it's too late.

While I am a strong proponent of men's groups, and have led one at my house every week for over 30 years, there is nothing that protects you from this attack from the enemy more than at least one close personal friend who you can tell anything to, that has your back, and who will be brutally honest when he notices something is slipping off the tracks. This watchman (or better if you can have a group of watchmen) is always looking out for you and your marriage and will quickly call it out when he sees the enemy sneaking over the hill.

The Outer Wall

Even though Hezekiah had repaired his walls and built watchtowers, he still directed his people to build "outer walls" - why? The reason is that if the watchmen fail (as they will) to see the approaching enemy (or you fail to believe them), and they get through your wall, there are catastrophic results - you lose your city and become a captive of the enemy. However, if you have outer walls, not only will the enemy be slowed down so that you have time to react and realize the true danger at hand, but, if breached, while bad, it is not catastrophic - you still have the main walls.

Similarly, men need outer walls built into their lives as protection against sexual temptation. Walls that, if breached, are bad, but don't lead to devastating results and help to wake us up to the more serious issue at hand before it's too late. Everyone should come up with his own outer walls with help from his wife or close friends if needed, but here are some I utilize in my own life. (1) Although you can't avoid noticing a beautiful woman either live or on a billboard as you walk through daily life, "I will make a covenant with my eyes not to look lustfully at a young woman" (Job 31:1), meaning that I will not dwell on another woman or image to the point of fantasizing about her sexually - this is the first step to falling into real sin; (2) Although I love to watch great shows and movies like all men, you need to be selective with what you expose yourself to, particularly if you find yourself seeking out shows or movies when you're alone because they might be sexual; (3) Don't ever flirt with another woman even if they are a friend and it seems totally innocent - flirting (meaning joking, or complimenting or being chivalrous when it gives you even a slight sexual buzz) with another woman is flirting with danger; (4) If you have to travel as part of your job and find yourself alone in a hotel room and can't sleep, resist the temptation to channel flip from boredom as you will just channel flip your way into temptation - don't eat in your room - go out and bring a book; and (5) be very careful with the internet, put on SafeSearch when you're felling strong, and stop any sexual rabbit trail in Twitter, Facebook, or Instagram.

Block the Water from the Enemy

One of the most beautiful descriptions Jesus gave of himself is found in John 4:13-14 when He compares earthly water to the "living water" found in Him to the woman at the well.

> "Jesus answered, 'Everyone who drinks this water will be thirsty again, but whoever drinks the water I give them will never thirst. Indeed, the water I give them will become in them a spring of water welling up to eternal life.'" (NIV)

However, water is not always symbolic for good things in scripture. If used by the enemy, it can destroy you. "Then from his mouth the serpent spewed water like a river, to overtake the woman and sweep her away with the torrent." (Rev. 12:15 NIV) Water is even used as a symbol for the deception of the enemy used to confuse us in our walk with God. "Reach down your hand from on high; deliver me and rescue me from the mighty waters, from the hands of the foreigners whose mouths are full of lies, whose right hands are deceitful." (Psalms 144:7-8 NIV)

Once completed, Hezekiah's Tunnel fed water from the now blocked Gihon Spring to the newly constructed Pool of Siloam so that water would remain behind the walls and not be used by the enemy against them. Siloam means to "be sent" or to "let go" from the Hebrew "shalah" and its pool (created from a decision to block the influence of the enemy) later became a place of healing in the time of Jesus.

> "After saying this, he spit on the ground, made some mud with the saliva, and put it on the man's eyes. 'Go,' he told him, 'wash in the Pool of Siloam' (this word means 'Sent'). So the man went and washed and came home seeing." (John 9:6-7 NIV)

As Christian men and leaders in the church we cannot just sit by and allow the enemy to drink from our water and overtake our home. We must rise up like Hezekiah, acknowledge the threat for what it is and take action. Only then can we let go and see clearly again.

♦ 14 ♦

The Pearl of Great Price

There it was - Kong Island! My friend Justin and I were so excited! We had been in Uganda for a week of prayer and work with my wife Libby, and we were so ready for an adventure. We had seen the island from our lunch spot on Lake Victoria near Entebbe where we had arrived hours before - an island about half a mile off the coast of the second largest fresh water lake in the world, with lush green foliage and who knows what else. So, in our adolescent glee (both a bit too old for), we ate our goat and chips and dreamed of somehow getting to the island at some point during our trip. It happened on the last day when we had returned from Gulu, had heard shocking and redemptive testimonies from escapees of the horrors of Joseph Kony at different churches in Kampala with our friends from World Vision, and were resting as we awaited our flight out the next day. We told our dream (now also shared by our new friend Patrick - who had risen up to be a high officer in Kony's army after being kidnapped as a young boy) with our dear friend Dan Gimadu (later to become Bishop Dan), an Anglican Priest who had journeyed with us to the North, and he told us that he would try. So, we took a very sweaty and smelly cab ride down to the Lake Victoria coast in search of a boat. Dan quickly found a willing fisherman who agreed to take us out to the island for 20,000 Ugandan Shillings (about $5.00) and we were off in our flea filled, carved out fishing boat - the lawyer, the 20 year old cameraman, the curious fisherman, the escaped child soldier and the Anglican Priest (in full garb no less).

As we approached the island (one of the 84 secluded clusters of islands off the shore called the Ssese Group), we saw huts on a beach on this tropical island with about 100 people waving to us eager for a visit from the priest and the Mzungu's. Then the fisherman said something in Bugandan to Dan and our plans changed. "Those are cannibals - maybe we should visit the other side of the island." Well, we went ashore on the other side of the island near a huge tree filled with exotic birds and our unlikely troop walked up to the crest of the hill only to quickly find a voodoo altar filled with freaky statues and money sacrifices. After Dan grabbed the money (to be transformed from evil to good), he prayed off all the evil spirits, wiped out the altar with a stick, and we were back in the boat heading to the mainland.

Then it happened. I've been in rainstorms before, but this was different - the sky just opened up and we were getting pummeled with rain. We Mzungus began hunkering down as Dan stood up in the boat, spread out his arms and in the loudest preacher voice he could muster from his 5'2" frame and shouted out, "Dear Lord - my friends have travelled so far to be here with us in Uganda - we love the rain, but not right now - in the name of Jesus - STOP!" Well, it did - immediately. My faith was strengthened. I had witnessed a true Biblestoryesque miracle. My first adventure in Uganda had come to an end, but the story was only beginning.

Our connection and ultimate love affair with Uganda (dubbed "The Pearl of Africa" by British colonists for its rich landscape and natural resources) began on a Sunday morning in the summer of 2005 when my wife Libby read a photo essay in the LA Times by Francine Orr chronicling the horrors occurring in Northern Uganda at the time. The pictures were heart wrenching. One, of a young woman named Lokerian Aciro who had had her lips and ears cut off by an 11 year old child soldier, was too much for my wife to handle. Something had to be done. As she researched a bit she learned that 30,000 children (primarily aged five to eleven - as this age of children was considered most impressionable) had been kidnapped, and that Northern Uganda now had the unwanted distinction of being UNICEF's worst place in the world to be a child in 2005.

Brain washed by the evil Joseph Kony, whose Lord's Resistance Army ("LRA") was terrorizing the North, these young child soldiers (chronicled in such documentaries as "The Invisible Children" and in the movie "Machine Gun Preacher") were kidnapped from their villages during the night, forced to kill or maim their family members, rubbed with magic oil to make them impervious to bullets, and then turned into killing machines, or in the sad case of many of the young women - sex slaves. The rise of Joseph Kony (an Acholi) is intriguing in light of the history of this nation which gained its independence (but not necessarily its freedom) from England in 1962.

England had been "awarded" the colony of Uganda during the division of Africa led by King Leopold of Belgium (chronicled in the excellent book "King Leopold's Ghost") and like many of the European colonists, used ethnic, territorial and economic division to aid in their governance of this new colony. During the colonial period, the British encouraged economic development in the South with the primarily Bugandan people group, but determined that the Acholi "tribe" (not really a tribe but an ethnic people living in the North) would serve as manual laborers as well as colonial police.

After three years under the fairly peaceful rule of Sir Edward Luwangula (placed in power with British influence - hence the "Sir"), Milton Obote (a Bugandan) came into power, but had no love for the North and would not bow to the influence of the British or American powers at the time. With the support of the British and Americans, the now infamous Idi Amin (an Acholi) then took power in 1971 and began a reign of insane terror best chronicled in the movie "The Last King of Scotland." With the world rising up against him after the famous "Raid on Entebbe" in which Israel commandos swooped over Lake Victoria to rescue Israeli passengers from a plane hijacked by the PLO and allowed to land in Uganda, there was another Western supported military coup.

This ultimately led to England and America holding their noses and allowing Obote to take power once again until deposed in 1985 by General Tito Okello soon to be followed by now President Yoweri Musevni.

When President Musevni (beloved in the West for his fight against AIDS and holder of the "peace" in Uganda) took power, he immediately ordered revenge killings in the North. Joseph Kony rose up in a Messianic rebellion against this "evil" government led by Musevni, started kidnapping children in the night creating thousands of "night commuters" who would travel at dusk from their villages to city centers (particularly in Gulu) to escape captivity by huddling in hospitals and government buildings before walking miles back to school the next morning. In response, Musevni began moving the Acholi people into government internment camps in 1999. This series of camps ultimately included 1.8 million Acholis living in small thatch-roofed mud huts squeezed together in a sea of humanity you had to see to believe. While the UN tried to help as they could, 1000 people were dying per week of disease and AIDS, and while "protected" from Kony, still suffered atrocities from Ugandan government soldiers. It was after 20 years of suffering in the North, with Kony on the run but still kidnapping children and night commuters still making the daily trek to Gulu (at this stage to a protected location by the NGO "Noah's Ark") that we found ourselves in this ravaged northern city in January of 2006.

After reading Francine Orr's photo essay, Libby began not only seeking out people in our community to pray, but searching for those around the world who were also praying for this horrific situation in Northern Uganda. In early December of 2005 she learned of Pastor Dennis Odoi who was the Minister of Prayer for World Vision in Uganda and began a relationship via e-mail. Pastor Odoi advised her that amazingly, the churches in southern Uganda were basically unaware of the atrocities in the North as the government was controlling the flow of information. World Vision was running a Child Rehabilitation Center in Gulu at the time and had the dream of bringing former child soldiers south to give their testimonies in churches in Kampala in an attempt to partner the southern churches with churches in the North. All they needed to fund this effort was $5,000. At the time we were attending Sandals Church in Riverside, California, and that Sunday in January 2006, the pastor announced that a woman in the church had approached him advising that the Lord had told her to give $10,000 to the church "for Africa". As Sandals didn't have an Africa ministry, the pastor just asked the church to pray. Well, Libby didn't need to pray, she just needed a dose of boldness to make the ask. After praying with my dad and TURN's executive director at the time, Anna Reyes, Libby marched into the office of Sandals' missions pastor and good friend TJ O'Donnell and told him of the need. Not only did TJ immediately approve the request, but he told Libby that because Sandals valued relationship, he didn't only want to send money, he wanted to send us to Uganda. So, five days later, packed with gifts for Pastor Dennis and his wife and kids, and with our spontaneous, adventurous young photographer friend Justin Pardee, we landed at Entebbe.

Upon meeting the wonderful Dennis Odoi and his wife Harriett, Pastor Dennis asked us, "Who's the preacher?" Justin and I quickly pointed to Libby and she did what you should always be prepared for when you visit Africa - started writing a sermon for church the next day. Not only did Libby preach to a church of about 200 people after we were introduced as the much honored Salongo ("father of twins") and his wife, but she "Africa" preached for about an hour and a half about our call to Uganda, the grace of God, and the power of being "Jesus with legs." Following the service, Dennis asked us to go to lunch with a woman he had met that day at church who needed to talk with us. As we ate our now beloved dish of fried whole tilapia, she told us how she had had a dream the night before that a woman in a white coat was coming to this church she had only been to once before, and that she was to collect clothes and shoes and bring them to church. Well, prior to the trip to Uganda, Libby called out to her friends for help in what to bring for her first trip to Africa. Her dear friend Joyce told her, "Whatever you do, just make sure to bring a white jacket as it will always come in handy in Africa." Of course she brought one, wore it that Sunday, and our new friend's prophetic dream came true and we took those clothes and shoes with us on our trip to the North.

We were then blessed to travel to Gulu with Dennis and "stop the rain" Dan. Our visit to the World Vision Rehab Center was both touching and troubling as we learned about the atrocities that these young men and women had experienced. But God is redemptive and even in the midst of horrific abuse, there was joy as we watched these now free children of God worship and the children born of war and abuse play and sing about Jesus. The internment camps are now gone, but the impact of so many people living for so long in such conditions has made an imprint on the North. When we arrived in Gulu we were surprised to see our new friend Florence (the one who prophesied over Austin the week before) who had been told by God to get on a bus and make the nearly five hour trek north to meet us. Pastor Florence ran a beautiful ministry to AIDS orphans, 15 of whom she was raising in her small home/church. Her story of dying, going to heaven, and then returning for a greater purpose, is one of those "only in Africa" stories, but as it was confirmed to us by so many people (all of whom call her Lazarus) and she actually acts like she went to heaven, I'm a believer.

As of the time of writing this chapter, I have been back to Uganda six times, the last being with my son Austin who was able to meet all our friends, particularly Florence who had so accurately prophesied over him 10 years earlier. Our relationship with Uganda now involves micro-finance loan programs for vulnerable women to help them be successful entrepreneurs, overseen by my daughter Becky and dear friends Brian and Ammabel, and my new adventure for next summer - working with the Global Justice Program at Pepperdine University helping cut plea deals for prisoners in three city prisons - one being back in Gulu where it all started for me. For all the good that God allows me to do in this beautiful nation, the impact on me and my family of spending time with these gracious, faithful, and loving people will last a lifetime and beyond. The adventure continues!

♦ 15 ♦

"Your Table is Ready!"

As I was growing up, it seemed as if my dad always had a wise thing to say to meet any situation I found myself in - a Godly perspective that I had never thought of before. Clearly most of this wisdom came from his love of the Bible, but one day I looked a little closer at his devotional reading and saw the book "My Utmost for His Highest" by Oswald Chambers. This amazing devotional was actually a compilation of his preaching to students and soldiers in the early 1900's from notes taken by his wife Gertrude (or "Biddy" as he called her). In 1935, almost 20 years after his untimely death at 43 years old, she got it published and it has been a Christian classic beloved by many to this day. My dad gave me a copy as I left for college and upon adding it to my daily reading, I realized that much of the fatherly wisdom from my dad actually came from Oswald Chambers who appears to ("read my mail") on a daily basis even though over 100 years ago. I still read "My Utmost" every day, share what I learn with friends and family (my kids call him Ozzy), and find inspiration and challenge even after reading a daily entry for what may be the 20th time.

One of my favorite days in "My Utmost" is March 20th which is entitled "Friendship With God" but really focuses on the concept of "God's Will" in our lives. We spend a lot of time praying and often worrying about whether we are in or out of "God's Will." Oswald Chambers deals with this issue from a more thoughtful perspective focusing not on God's intended will or plan for our lives, but rather on our friendship with God.

> "To be so much in contact with God that you never need to ask Him to show you His will, is to be nearing the final stage of your discipline in the life of faith. When you are rightly related to God, it is a life of

> freedom and liberty and delight, you *are* God's will, and all your commonsense decisions are His will for you unless He checks. You decide things in perfect delightful friendship with God, knowing that if your decisions are wrong He will always check; when He checks, stop at once."

The truth that we ARE God's will when we live in a state of constant communion with him has been extremely freeing for my life even though tested at times when life's challenges come crashing down. It is during these difficult times in my life - many of which are outlined in this book - that I must stay close to God, must keep reading His word, must keep praying, must keep in community. If I don't, then, whether in good times or bad, I will risk falling out of God's plan for my life and rather, fall into making decisions based upon pride, or fear, or greed, or lust.

Jeremiah 29:11 is an oft quoted scripture to encourage those going through hard times as the prophet declares, "'I know the plans I have for you,' declares the Lord, 'plans to prosper you and not to harm you, plans to give you hope and a future." (NIV) While true, the context is important. This is a "Letter to the Exiles" in Babylon and states in 29:10, "When seventy years are completed for Babylon, I will come to you and fulfill my good promise to bring you back to this place." So, while verse 11 is so hopeful, verse 10 reminds us that Israel's captivity was going to last for 70 years. I don't fully understand God's timing, or how his plan works with His people on this fallen planet, but what I do know is that even in the darkest times, when all hope is lost, when things appear impossible, there is always hope! It may take some time (hopefully not 70 years), but if we stay close to Him, and live in hope, we will live the abundant life and many times see miracles in our lives.

I love my wife so much not only because she is beautiful and smart and funny, but because she ALWAYS has hope. Even in our darkest days, she KNEW good (no GREAT) was coming! The epitome of her hopeful nature came one evening in Santa Barbara as we had run out of money, had our house up for sale, didn't know what we were going to do next, but had decided to travel to Alabama to be at our daughter's track meet even though we couldn't afford it. Libby's 50th birthday was approaching and I had secretly planned a surprise party for her that next week, so when she told me that ALL she wanted for her birthday was a sunset cruise in the Santa Barbara Harbor that we had seen for many years but had never done, and perhaps split a fish dinner at Murphy Brothers restaurant in the harbor, I went with it. We dressed in our finest and hit the harbor right before sunset.

After a delightful cruise filled with hors d'oeuvres, Manhattans, and a beautiful sunset over Santa Barbara, we walked ashore to go to dinner at Murphy Brothers. The problem was that it was a Friday night in the summer and it was packed out. If you can believe it, when we asked how long the wait was they told us it was an hour and a half for indoor seating and a whopping two hours if we wanted (which we did) outdoor seating with a view of the harbor. Since it was already 8:30 pm, this was just not going to work, so we headed down the wharf as Libby declared "Don't worry, we're fine, it will all work out!" About 200 yards down the wharf was the bathroom right next door to another restaurant that was mainly burgers so didn't quite fit the bill for our romantic dressed up early 50th birthday faith dinner - but we were desperate, so as Libby hit the women's room, I checked in with the hostesses who had a kiosk outside.

After ten minutes, Libby approached carrying a restaurant buzzer that was lighting up and actually speaking the words "Your table is ready," "Your table is ready!" It appears that someone had left it at the water fountain outside the woman's restroom and she had heard it go off over and over as she was inside. Not sure why, but confident the buzzer had been abandoned, she picked it up and brought it over to the hostess to turn in. When the burger place hostess announced that it was not their buzzer, but rather from the fancy restaurant down the wharf called Murphy Brothers, Libby's spirit kicked it and she ran back yelling "Quick, follow me!" with the buzzer still yelling "Your table's ready!" Of course, being the wimpy one, I let her run up the restaurant steps and check it out fearing embarrassment and just being shocked at her boldness. Well, she walked up to the Murphy Brothers hostess, presented her buzzer and the waitress actually said "Two right?" - "Yes" - "Outside right?" - "Of course" and lo and behold when I walked up the steps, my wife was sitting outside in the best seat in the house only 15 minutes after we had initially checked in.

The rest is a bit of history as going to Becky's National Championship (which ended up being fully paid for by the coach - of course) not only meant being part of an amazing time in our daughter's life, but it paved the way for our decision to rent (and therefore keep) our house, move to Poway, California, and begin a chapter in our life which I can honestly say was impossible to even imagine. I really feel like God had been screaming to us that "Your table is ready!" but we needed to wait and have hope, stay close to Him, and when the time came - step out in faith and grab what He had for us - something way more fun and fulfilling than anything we could have planned for ourselves - His Will!

The Puzzle

Claren Wallace Collier – 2015

There is a worldwide puzzle

broken in pieces by sin.

The only way to solve it

is putting it in God's hand.

Scattered by frustration,

in despair as we look,

from our broken state

for a picture to appear.

A prayer of surrender

to have them come together

a little at a time.

Events and circumstances

begin a way to find a person or event

to surprise us once again.

Give us the joy of an answer

yet unknown before.

As piece by piece the puzzle forms

into the planned design

that opens up a way for more.

The picture shown excites us,

becomes a joy to see.

God's will that was waiting

for what He wanted all along.

www.ingramcontent.com/pod-product-compliance
Lightning Source LLC
Chambersburg PA
CBHW060357050426
42449CB00009B/1782

9780692968741